TRAINING IN SMA...
A Study of Five Methods

Other Titles of Interest:

DAY P R:
Communication in Social Work

DAY P R:
Methods of Learning Communication Skills

HEAP K:
Group Theory for Social Workers

HERAUD B J:
Sociology and Social Workers

KAHN J H:
Human Growth & The Development of Personality, 2nd Edition

MUNRO A & McCULLOCH W:
Psychiatry for Social Workers

PHILIP A E *et al*:
Social Work Research and the Analysis of Social Data

THOMPSON S & KAHN J H:
The Group Process as a Helping Technique

TILBURY D E F
Casework in Context: A Basis for Practice

TRAINING IN SMALL GROUPS:
A Study of Five Methods

Edited by

B. BABINGTON SMITH, OBE, MA.
Formerly Senior Lecturer in Experimental Psychology, Oxford University

and

B. A. FARRELL, MA, B LITT.
Reader in Mental Philosophy, Oxford University

PERGAMON PRESS
OXFORD · NEW YORK · TORONTO · SYDNEY · PARIS · FRANKFURT

U.K.	Pergamon Press Ltd., Headington Hill Hall, Oxford OX3 OBW, England
U.S.A.	Pergamon Press Inc., Maxwell House, Fairview Park, Elmsford, New York 10523, U.S.A.
CANADA	Pergamon of Canada, Suite 104, 150 Consumers Road, Willowdale, Ontario, M2J 1P9, Canada
AUSTRALIA	Pergamon Press (Aust.) Pty. Ltd., P.O. Box 544, Potts Point, N.S.W. 2011, Australia
FRANCE	Pergamon Press SARL, 24 rue des Ecoles, 75240 Paris, Cedex 05, France
FEDERAL REPUBLIC OF GERMANY	Pergamon Press GmbH, 6242 Kronberg-Taunus, Pferdstrasse 1, Federal Republic of Germany

Copyright © 1979. B. Babington Smith and B. A. Farrell

All Rights Reserved. No part of this publication may be reproduced, stored in a retrieval system or transmitted in any form or by any means: electronic, electrostatic, magnetic tape, mechanical, photocopying, recording or otherwise, without permission in writing from the publishers

First edition 1979

British Library Cataloguing in Publication Data
Training in groups.
1. Group relations training —
I. Babington Smith, Bernard II, Farrell, Brian Anthony
301.11   HM134   79-40425
ISBN 0-08-023689-8

Printed and bound at William Clowes & Sons Limited Beccles and London

PERGAMON PRESS GRATEFULLY ACKNOWLEDGES THE
ASSISTANCE OF THE COVERDALE ORGANISATION
IN THE PUBLICATION OF THIS BOOK.

To the memory of
RALPH COVERDALE AND PIERRE TURQUET

Contents

Preface	The Editors	xi
Introduction	B. Babington Smith, OBE, MA. Formerly Senior Lecturer in Experimental Psychology and Fellow of Pembroke College, Oxford University.	1
Chapter 1	**Training Leaders** John Adair, PhD, B Litt. Consultant and author.	5
Chapter 2	**Coverdale Training** John Waterston, BA. World Bank, Washington D.C., U.S.A. Formerly Consultant, Coverdale Training Ltd.	19
Chapter 3	**The Study of the Small Group in an Organisational Setting** B. W. M. Palmer, MA. Consultant, The Grubb Institute of Behavioural Studies.	41
Chapter 4	**Small Group Work in a Psychiatric Prison** B. Marcus, BA. Principal Psychologist, H.M. Prison, Grendon.	62
Chapter 5	**Small Group Work in Relation to Management Development** K. B. Low, BA. Director of Studies, Ecole des Affaires de Paris, Oxford. Formerly Management Development Adviser, Philips Industries Ltd. and H. Bridger, TD, BSc., Dip. Ed. Programme Director, Career Development and Institutional Change, Tavistock Institute of Human Relations. Social Science Adviser, Philips Industries Ltd.	83
Chapter 6	**Work in Small Groups: Some Philosophical Considerations** B. A. Farrell, MA, B Litt. Fellow of Corpus Christi College, Reader in Mental Philosophy, Oxford University.	103

Chapter 7	*Some Psychological and Practical Considerations* By B. Babington Smith.	116
Postscripts		133
Name Index		137
Subject Index		139

Preface

The seeds of this book were sown in 1970 when the Editors organised a seminar at Oxford in the then Institute of Experimental Psychology with the title 'Methods and Experiences in Small Groups'.

Both editors had experience with small group work, Mr. Farrell in connection with logical aspects of psychoanalytic claims and Mr. Babington Smith in working with Mr. R. Coverdale in developing the methods which have come to be known by his name. Both felt that undergraduates, in their reading and even in laboratory work, could form no adequate idea of the range of applications or methods or variety of human experience to be found in small group work. The seminar was designed to let undergraduates hear from a number of practitioners in person about their methods and their work.

The design of the eight meetings of the seminar need not be described in detail, but it included talks by the editors and five British practitioners, Dr. P. M. Turquet, Mr. H. Bridger, Mr. R. Coverdale, Dr. J. E. Adair, and Mr. B. Marcus. When the seminar was over it was suggested that the outside speakers, none of whom had heard what the others had to say, should meet. Two such meetings were held in Oxford, which were of great interest in showing the difficulty in reaching understanding, let alone agreement, on basic ideas. Out of these meetings came the proposal for a book to present something of the variety of approaches and of ideas among practitioners in the field of small groups.

The book was designed to give readers something that did not exist: a presentation by a number of British practitioners of what they set out to do in training in small groups, how they set about it and what they thought they achieved, in such a form that comparisons of ideas and methods could be made. Much had been written and published about various methods (chiefly American and chiefly kinds of T-group), but there was little in the way of material for a comparative study. While some serious attempts to assess results quantitatively have been published, practitioners may well feel that what they achieve is not to be conveyed in numbers, or that it slips through a grid of cross-classification.

Collecting written chapters from busy men is probably never easy. Three of the original five speakers encountered such difficulties that the editors agreed to a colleague writing or assisting in the writing of a chapter. Where this has happened we have asked the incoming writer to present his own view of the work; Mr. Bridger, one of the original speakers, appears as second author with Mr. Low.

The five chapters of the book are followed by two commentaries, one each by the editors, who have not seen it as part of their editorial function to engage in argument between themselves. They wish to make it clear that neither editor regards himself as being committed to statements made by the other. Mr. Farrell considers some philosophical issues, adopting a theoretical approach which points to practical and educational implications. In the last chapter Mr. Babington Smith, concentrating on psychological aspects, makes comparison of the five methods, and then turns to the question of appraising them and their achievements.

It is only fair to readers (and to the authors) to explain that to keep within publisher's requirements, and in the interests of readers' purses, the five chapters and the editors' commentaries have been severely limited in length, and that the five authors were not invited to rewrite their contribution in terms of any recent developments.

Since the original chapters were put in hand there have been important developments in the field, such as encounter groups, 'Gestalt', synectics, and other methods which have reached this country mainly from America. To have attempted to include chapters about them would have cut across the plan of presenting only British work and would have meant extending the scope of this book to cover methods which are at least as much concerned with individual development as with group behaviour. Nevertheless we have found the contributors welcoming an opportunity to indicate recent developments in their work. These postscripts are printed together after Chapter 7.

It is very sad that two of the speakers in the original symposium, Ralph Coverdale and Dr. P. M. Turquet, both died in 1975. Each had done very valuable work and each was a leader in his own particular field.

Mr. Babington Smith takes this opportunity of acknowledging a great personal debt to Ralph Coverdale for introducing him to, and for enabling him to work in, the field of small groups. Mr. Farrell wishes to acknowledge his great indebtedness to the work of Dr. Turquet and for the help he received from him. Finally Mr. Farrell and Mr. Babington Smith have great pleasure in acknowledging that, after the book had reached its present form, The Coverdale Organisation freely offered generous backing, thus enabling the publication of the book to proceed, but naturally is neither responsible for nor committed to any of the views expressed by the authors or editors.

B. BABINGTON SMITH
B. A. FARRELL
Editors

Introduction
BY B. BABINGTON SMITH

There can be no doubt of the great growth and proliferation of small group methods of training since 1945. Not only has the number of participants, i.e. of people being trained, grown, but so also has the number of practitioners, the variety of methods offered and the volume of published matter. It was estimated in 1968 that, starting from an effective zero in 1947, the number of people experiencing such training had reached 150,000: since then the number has continued to grow at an increasing rate. Carl Rogers[1] for instance, writes 'A well informed leader in the field estimates privately that during 1970 750,000 individuals will participate in some type of intensive group experience'. While there is no way to check the accuracy of this figure, it would seem a reasonable guess. The method has spread from the United States and Great Britain to Japan, India, countries in Western Europe and to South Africa. In Great Britain alone the number having experience of small group training could now be nearing five figures annually. Such growth over 25 years is evidence of some power or attraction in small group work striking enough to call for explanation. It would indeed be an ambitious claim that an explanation is offered here, but the contents of the book are organised to help the reader to a better understanding.

1. Historically four main sources of ideas and methods may be distinguished.
   (a) The use of small groups in psychotherapy, which goes back at least as far as the early 1930s, when they were first introduced in New York by Slavson[2] after what he describes as a serendipitous discovery of their value.
   (b) A good deal of group work has arisen in attempts to apply ideas from research by Social Psychologists. Most of the research in this field is American and it has been amply reported, e.g. Hare Borgatta & Bales.[3] In practical applications, such as Lewin's, concern centred chiefly on group dynamics; that is on patterns of interplay between individuals.
   (c) Other work derived from sociological ideas, mainly about organisational theory, which is concerned primarily with the nature of groups and their interactions, including their interactions within organisations.
   (d) That form of milieu therapy usually called the therapeutic community.

The latter term was first used in 1946 by T.F. Main[4] of work done at Northfields Military Hospital during the war. About this time Maxwell Jones[5] was quite independently doing similar work that also grew out of war-time experience of psychotherapy.

In all psychotherapy there is an implication that something is wrong: therapy is concerned with putting it right, or at least making things less wrong. In Social Psychology and in Sociology, academic work is concerned with the nature of group phenomena and their implications, not with their rightness or desirability. One must notice, however, that the names of characteristics discussed are often socially or politically loaded (e.g. 'authoritarian' or 'democratic'). The foregoing points are important; for when one enters the field of practical affairs, different values and different criteria are found to obtain. It cannot safely be assumed that academic findings and methods will be relevant or useful.

By the end of the Second World War evidence had accumulated (for instance, in Bion and Rickman's work[6] with small groups of patients in the British Army, and in work by Lewin[7] in the U.S.A.) of the power of small groups to produce changes in people.

2. With the organisation in 1947 of the National Training Laboratories (N.T.L.) in the U.S.A. by Leland Bradford and others, small group work emerged (from therapy and research) as an educative or training method. The first training laboratories were held at Bethel, Maine that year, shortly after Kurt Lewin's death, but much indebted to his ideas. It was at Bethel under N.T.L. that the T-group method and sensitivity training started and developed. The term T-group and its near-synonym sensitivity training have become ominous for some people with hints of scarifying experiences and emotional ordeals. Originally, and as used by its practitioners, T-group is intended to mean simply a group that meets for purposes of training under controlled conditions; sensitivity training is directed to improving perception of others and heightening awareness of one's own feelings and of the feelings of others.

In Great Britain, at the Tavistock Institute, Bion had started the small groups on the basis of which he wrote *Experience in Small Groups*[8] setting out his formulation of the ways in which such groups function.

In 1957, a seminal date for small group work in this country, the Tavistock Institute and Leicester University ran a conference at Leicester.

A striking feature of small group work at this time was the 'leaderless' or 'unstructured' group. A small number of people brought together received an 'open' instruction such as 'form a group', or even no overt instruction. There would be a member (or members) of the staff present, but participants would find that he neither led them nor responded to questions in a way that could be seen as helpful. As with much else in the situation, it was by design left to the participants to discover, from such responses as they received from the staff, what form of help they could expect to receive.

The Therapeutic Community, while larger in size and including people who were known to be doctors and nurses, involved a similar flattening of structure, by which phrase is meant that, though people known to be doctors and nurses were present, they were found not to be exercising their authority or making contributions from their knowledge or experience, in any ordinary sense, in such a way as to lighten the difficulties of the situation for the patients or lay members of the group. By this means everyone was forced to face their responsibilities and come to appreciate how they could contribute to the functioning of the community.

The experience of an unstructured group is for most people not easily forgotten. Growing puzzlement can be fended off for a time with conversation or silence, but a state of deep frustration is reached as the group, failing to elicit helpful response from staff members, finds itself unable to make sense of its situation. It is a characteristic of frustration that when a way out is found or an insight dawns, it is succeeded by elation. The state of euphoria and enthusiasm in a small group that has made such a discovery can be a memorable experience. Growing experience has shown, however, that the structureless group is very time-consuming, and in fact all methods described here now use situations that are structured to some extent.

3. From this stage there have been several lines of development in Great Britain, with different practitioners moving in different directions from the leaderless group.

In the development of the Tavistock courses, as described by Rice,[9] emphasis shifted towards 'leadership'. Conflict was courted if not encouraged; a line justified on the basis that since conflict is inevitable, it is important to recognise the behaviour of others and one's own feelings in situations of conflict, so as to be able to understand and deal with conflict later. The methods described in this book by Palmer and by Low are derived, along separate lines, from the work of the Tavistock. Both describe ways in which groups can escape from the unstructured situation by focussing attention — with consistent support from the staff — on 'the here and now' (what is happening now in the group) and on this basis can develop useful understanding of structure. An important difference between them is that Low emphasises the understanding of 'process' in the group as a means to effective teamwork, while Palmer focusses interest on the study of authority and on improvement in taking roles.

Waterston describes the different line of development taken by Coverdale Training. The early lesson that open instructions led to frustration and the view that the concern of business men is to 'get things done' led to a much greater emphasis by Coverdale on looking forward, on clarity of aims and better planning. Two points to note are, first that only if plans are put into action is the responsibility they imply actually shouldered, and secondly, that only if action is reviewed can lessons be drawn to improve performance. Between them these points gave action its central position in Coverdale Training. In this method leadership is seen as one feature of teamwork.

Leadership is the central theme of Adair's method. Adair, himself a qualified N.T.L. trainer, has judged the T-group more suitable for the U.S.A. than for Great Britain. In the setting of R.M.C., Sandhurst he had the opportunity to give shape to his ideas and devised a method for studying and inculcating leadership in small groups using inductive, exploratory and cooperative methods. The situations are well structured, to the point that there is little for the staff to do. The concentration in one area, leadership, allows great compactness of design and a total duration of a day and a half.

Marcus's work, like that of the others, involves working with small groups. The therapeutic community from which his method is derived is medically orientated, but it is clear from Marcus's account that he has taken deliberate steps to play down any medical overtones. It is fair to regard this method as another divergent development from an original concern with an unstructured group.

What I have tried to show above is that the confluence of several streams in small group work turned an extremely powerful psychological situation, that of the leaderless group, into an exciting educational tool, the T-group. With use this was found to require modification and, in course of time, different lines of development from a structureless group have been followed by different practitioners, in the general direction of increasing structure. It is still true that the term T-group is very widely used and the greater part of the literature about small group work is about T-groups. None of the authors of the five chapters that follow admits to working with T-groups as such; though as clearly indicated most of these methods are derived, at least in part, from work with T-groups.

In some of these methods of helping people in their interpersonal relations there has been a trend to greater concern with the development of techniques and skills and a lessening of emphasis on learning by discovery and insight. There are at least two sound practical reasons for so doing. A 'perpetual spring' of induction and discovery is very exhausting and, as staff become more familiar with likely group situations, the manipulative aspect of 'conducted tours' of exploration can become obtrusive.

References

1. Rogers, Carl, *Encounter Groups* (1973), Pelican, p. 151.
2. Slavson, S. R., *A textbook in analytic group psychotherapy* (1964), New York: International Universities Press.
3. Hare, P. A.; Borgatta, E.; Bales, R. F., *Small Groups: a study in social interaction* (1965), New York: Alfred A. Knopf.
4. Main, T. F., 'The hospital as a therapeutic institution', *Bull. Menninger Clinic* (1946), vol. 10, p. 66.
5. Jones, Maxwell *et al.*, *Social Psychiatry, a study of therapeutic communities* (1952), London: Tavistock Publications.
6. Bion, W. R.; Rickman, J., 'Intra-group Tensions in Therapy', *Lancet* (1943), vol. II, p. 678.
7. Lewin, K., *Group decisions and social change. Readings in Social Psychology* (1947), Ed. Newcomb and Hartley.
8. Bion, W. R., *Experiences in Small Groups* (1961), London: Tavistock Publications.
9. Rice, A. K., *Learning for leadership* (1965), London: Tavistock Publications.

CHAPTER 1

Training Leaders

BY JOHN ADAIR

The need for good leadership has come to be widely accepted during this generation in every sphere of working life. Some professions, such as the military services, have used the word 'leadership' unstintingly for many decades, but now it has acquired a general currency in industry, commerce and the public services as a whole. But the central problem has become how to develop a sufficient supply of good leaders to meet the requirements of the contemporary situation. One answer to that problem is to devise new methods of training leaders, or—more accurately—to improve those methods which societies have always traditionally evolved for fostering the precious resource of leadership. This chapter is a description of some experiments along those lines.

From 1961 until 1964 I was engaged upon research into the content and methods of leadership training, work undertaken as a voluntary adjunct to my duties as a Lecturer in Military History at the Royal Military Academy, Sandhurst. As a result of these studies and many discussions with my military colleagues, a $1\frac{1}{2}$ day Functional Leadership Course was accepted in 1964, and all officer cadets underwent it that year. Subsequently all the Royal Air Force and some Royal Navy schools for officers and non-commissioned officers took over the course, and a number of industrial firms followed suit in the period from 1968 onwards, not least owing to the energetic espousal of the Industrial Society. By the time of writing (1972) over 50,000 managers and supervisors have undergone Action-Centred Leadership (ACL) training, to give it the name which the Industrial Society invented in 1968.

The Small Group Approach

A particular feature of this course, in its military or industrial settings, is the participative educational method. The matrix for this greater use of the discussion group was the movement which came to be known as Group Dynamics in America during the 1930s, whose best-known pioneer and exponent was Kurt Lewin. ACL has come to differ from the more direct linear descendants of the Group Dynamics movement and it is important to grasp how this has come about.

Historical research would perhaps show that originally the 'leaderless' or 'unstructured' group meeting over 2 weeks was employed as a *research* method. Early on, however, the increased awareness or sensitivity of the participants recommended Group Dynamics courses as training instruments, and the T-Group (Training Group) proper was born during the 1940s. Those organising T-Groups, and the Group Laboratories which included them as their central feature, often claimed that they produced a variety of changes in their members, such as greater sensitivity, enhanced skills (of various kinds) and improved leadership. Over 2 weeks a number of methods were used to these ends alongside the T-Groups of 16–20 people, each with a 'trainer' and one or two 'observers' (or associate trainers). These other methods included plenary lectures and films, intergroup exercises and paired interviews. The uniqueness of the T-Group approach was the emphasis it placed upon group discussion as the major method of change. The talks or 'theory sessions', for example, were seen as ancillary to the T-Groups, which occupied most of the time-table. This approach was well suited to the aim of giving each participant a sense of the forces, powers or 'dynamics' present in all groups. Its distinction between knowledge *about* (theoretical, second-hand) and knowledge *of* (experience, discovery), and exaltation of the latter, was a natural corollary to the group-centred approach to learning.

A major simple discovery of Group Dynamics was that the group was a much more powerful influence for producing change in an individual's attitudes or beliefs than a lecture, especially when the group as a whole made a decision to have its members change their behaviour. As such this characteristic of groups is a descriptive or amoral factor. It could be argued that the end justifies the means. The use of Group Dynamics, for example, by the Chinese to break down and 'brain-wash' United Nations prisoners in the Korean War could be called clearly 'bad', while the use to dilute so-called autocratic attitudes in managers or Church leaders might be thought to be manifestly 'good'. The consideration of 'ends' is indeed one vital element in the morality, but another one—sometimes neglected—is the safeguarding of the individual as an end in himself, not as a subordinate to the group. This last consideration sets a limit on the deployment of group pressure to ensure conformity, namely when the value of the individual is at stake.

The tendency to place an almost absolute value on the group at the expense of the individual person, coupled with a low estimate—amounting sometimes to disregard—of the all-pervading influence of the *situation* on relations between leader and others within a group or organisation, diminished the usefulness of Group Dynamics as a course for leadership training. But its accumulation of theories, models, methods and lore was a rich source of supply for those designing such courses.

In order to be in a position to enable others to learn more about good leadership the trainer needs not only an understanding of the various methods of education available, but also a grasp of the research into the content of his subject. For ACL training does include the transmission of some knowledge. It is based on the assumption that each of the main research approaches towards the understanding of leadership contains some truth which course participants will find both interesting and relevant to their responsibilities. In ACL these approaches are summed up in the trefoil model (p. 9), but the course members are also given the outline story of research, more-or-less along the following lines.

The Qualities Approach

The assumption behind this line of research was that men and women are either born with the silver spoon of leadership in their mouths or not, with a corollary that those who possess the inborn or inherent qualities of a leader will naturally emerge as the head of any group in which they are placed, regardless of the situation. They are born to lead.

The earliest research workers in this field tended to share this assumption that leadership consists of a certain pattern of inherited or acquired personality traits, and therefore they set about trying to produce a definitive list of qualities. Much to their surprise they found very little agreement among the many writers upon the topic. Each list seemed to be subjective, telling the reader more about the author's own temperament and beliefs than leadership.

One survey of twenty experimental studies, for example, revealed that only 5 per cent of the qualities examined were common to four or more studies.[1] In fact there was a bewildering number of trait names from which the student of leadership could make up his portfolio. Two researchers compiled a list of some 17,000 words for describing personality.[2]

Even if we seize on the lowest common denominator, the traits which appear in most lists, they tell us little about leadership. 'Courage' and 'initiative', for example, both favourites in almost any trait analysis of military leadership, are really qualities expected in all soldiers regardless of rank. They are essential military virtues. But it is quite possible to recall brave and resourceful soldiers who are not leaders by any stretch of the imagination.

The lack of agreement on the so-called leadership traits has tended to discredit this approach. Before leaving it, however, it is worth pointing out one undoubted truth which it portrays, namely that *leaders tend or ought to possess and exemplify the qualities or values esteemed by the group.* The leader has a symbolic or representative role which can perhaps best be understood in terms of qualities. This is especially true for national leaders. In the Second World War, for example, no small part of Winston Churchill's effectiveness lay in his power to portray vividly in words and appearance the sterling quality of the British nation at that time: bulldog resolve.

By its very nature the theory tended to lay the emphasis on leadership selection rather than training. Opinions varied as to how far the student could develop leadership qualities by the exercise of will power, but those who attempted this self-improvement found it extremely difficult. Indeed both psychologists and theologians suggest to us that such endeavours are largely self-defeating. It is hard to imagine, for example, how the conscious cultivation of a sense of humour can be anything but serious! Often the sole results of these frontal assaults upon leadership qualities was increased self-centredness—the one certain disqualification for leadership. From the leadership trainer's point of view, however, there is no reason to regret the disfavour into which the *qualities* approach has fallen.

The Situational Approach

A second theory may be called the *situational* approach. Those who held it believed that whoever became the leader in a small group depended upon the situation in which it found itself, including the task immediately confronting it. One investigator, who reviewed 74 studies in military leadership, concluded:

Leadership is specific to the particular situation under investigation . . . (there are) wide variations in the characteristics of individuals who become leaders in similar situations and even greater divergencies in leadership behaviour in different situations . . . The only common factor appeared to be that leaders in a particular field need and tend to possess superior general or technical competence or knowledge in that area.[3]

Further research into leadership, however, while confirming the main findings of the 'situationalists', also discovered a more general competence which was not so dependent upon the actual situation or group. This, the third theory of approach, may be called the *functional* understanding of leadership.

The Functional Approach

The best way to grasp the functional approach is to look for a moment at the *needs* in the life of any small group. There are present in the life of working groups three areas of need at any given time. First there is the need relating to the common task. One of the reasons why a group comes together is that there is a task which one person cannot do on his own. If you have a task to do which is not achieved—for instance, if you take some people to climb a mountain and forget to bring the guidebook, pitons and ropes, and get halfway up the mountain before this fact is discovered, the group will evince various signs of frustration, which will probably be vented on the leader. These are symptoms of a need present all the time in the group to complete the common purpose.

Secondly, and related to the task, there is a need which became known at Sandhurst as the need for 'team maintenance'; i.e. a need for a group to be held together as a working team so that it can achieve its purposes. This aspect the social psychologists have sometimes called 'group cohesiveness'.

Thirdly, individuals bring into the group their own needs; not just the physical ones for food and shelter, which are largely catered for by the payment of wages these days, but also their psychological needs; recognition, a sense of doing something worthwhile; status; the deeper needs to give to and receive from other people in a working situation. These personal needs are perhaps more profound than we sometimes realise.

These areas affect each other, as the model of three over-lapping circles suggests. To look at it negatively, if you have a group which does not achieve its task, then this will tend to affect the team maintenance area; disruptive tendencies may increase, morale will go down, and individual work satisfaction will also be affected. If the personal relationships within a group are bad, this may affect even the performance of the task and the need satisfaction of the individual members. Conversely, if a group achieves its tasks, then morale tends to become higher.

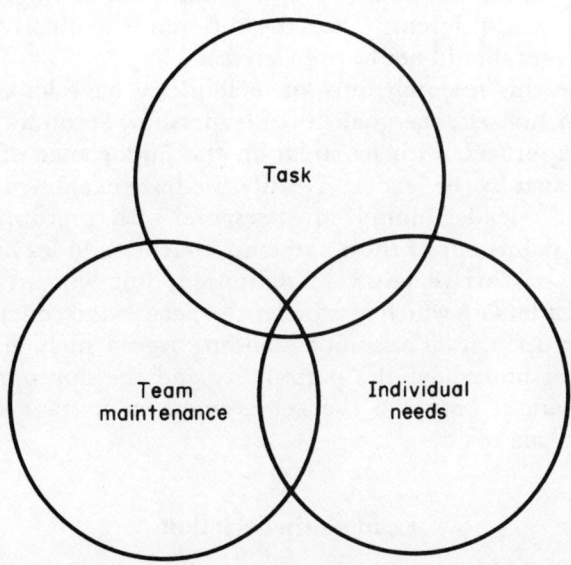

Inter-action of Group Needs

What has this to do with leadership? In order that the task shall be achieved, the group held together as a working team, and that individuals should feel that their own personal needs are met, the leader has to perform certain functions. In relation to the task, for example, he has to define it clearly, make a plan, allocate work to individuals, control activity on the job, and evaluate the performance. These are all functions which have to be performed in and for that group if it is to achieve its common aim. In the team maintenance area he has to set and maintain standards of discipline. Discipline in this sense can be best understood as the invisible bonds which bind a group together. He has to reconcile any differences which may threaten to diminish the harmony and the working efficiency of that group as a team. In the individual area he has to be aware of any particular problems which may affect the performance of a member on the common task and in relationships with others in the group.

The degree to which the leader shares these functions with members of his group varies according to the organisation and its purposes. A critical factor which influences, for example, how far he shares decision-making with members of his group is the time available in the situation in which he has to work especially where human life is also at risk. In situations where swift decisions are a matter of life and death, then organisations usually place in the hands of the leader the bulk of the decision-making function. Industrial leaders, by contrast with military ones, do not usually operate in such life-and-death situations and therefore it is often possible for a manager to share decisions much more readily with members of his group.[4] Yet the time factor may be just as pressing in industrial and commercial settings; it is the consequences which are different. Thus the difference in this respect between officer and manager should not be over-stressed.

To summarise this research into leadership, we have looked first at the individual leader himself, the qualities of leadership. Secondly we have noted the situational approach with its stress on the importance of the technical knowledge possessed by the leader. Thirdly, we have examined the needs in a group to which the leader himself must respond with appropriate functions. Taking the best points out of those three approaches and leaving out the less useful ones, we can arrive not at a definition, but we can reach an understanding of leadership which is sufficiently specific and concrete to allow us to base training upon it. That understanding would include the following points: the leader must have the personality and the appropriate technical knowledge to guide a group to the achievement of its task and to hold it together as a working team.

Leadership Selection

As long ago as 1942 the functional approach was applied to the problems of officer selection. In 1942 the then Adjutant-General found that the interview method, whereby a selector tried to spot the leadership qualities in candidates, was resulting sometimes in a 50 per cent failure rate at OCTUs, and as a consequence he brought together a highly gifted team to evolve a better method of selection. The results of this experiment, recorded in Dr. Henry Harris's book *The Group Approach to Leadership Testing* (1949), show the advantage of a method of selection in which the candidate is put in a group with a task to perform, and selected on the basis of his ability to provide the functions necessary to achieve that aim and to hold the group together as a working team. This method was adopted not only in all the Services of this country and many abroad, but it was also influential in industry. It is one which has produced good results consistently in the British Army for over 30 years.

Despite the success of the group approach to leadership selection, the principles behind it were not applied to the development of leaders in the Armed Services before 1963. At about that time, when I was a member of the staff of the Royal Military Academy, Sandhurst, it happened that I was asked to apply my knowledge of the content and methods of the group training which had already emerged to the work of improving the content and methods already employed to train 1000 Sandhurst Officer Cadets during their 2-year course. Only a year or so after the first experimental functional leadership course did I come to realise how close this form of training stood to the much earlier selection boards as described by Dr. Harris and others.

Functional Leadership Training at Sandhurst: Early Developments

In order to appreciate the contribution which functional leadership training was designed to make to the development of the young officer it is necessary to describe the basic organisation of Sandhurst.

Each of the twelve companies at that time were divided horizontally into three or four 'intakes'. A company 'intake' was therefore 18–24 officer cadets. In 1961 each intake received a dozen or so lectures based on the qualities approach to leadership, delivered by the company commander and followed by discussion. Field exercises, some as long as 10 days, touched only on the technical side, rarely on the leadership aspect. Yet the main purpose of Sandhurst, at that time as now, was to develop the leadership potential in each officer cadet.

We did some careful evaluation of this type of training with Intake 30. One hundred and fifty cadets took part in this survey and we found that in terms of figures, 14 per cent found it 'useful', 36 per cent found it 'of some use', 25 per cent found it 'of little use' and 25 per cent found it to be 'useless'. So out of those figures we could deduce that all but 14 per cent were not really getting very much out of the leadership instruction in this form, and the 14 per cent who did included those in least need of it — if the fact that most of them were holders of cadet ranks, such as under-officer, is evidence that they had already established their leadership ability.

During the period between 1962 and 1964 I had taken part in T-Group training in America, and 'graduated' eventually as a fully-fledged trainer. Also I had the opportunity of studying the varying extents to which military academies in the United States and Canada, France and the Scandinavian countries, had adopted the Group Dynamics approach, and with what results. Lastly, I had the experience of being a trainer in three T-Groups, composed respectively of English clergymen and laymen, an international group of Anglican bishops, and staff-members of British Colleges of Education. From these years I gathered some provisional conclusions about T-Group methods.

The drawbacks of T-Groups from the British Army's point of view would have been two-fold. First, military groups usually had a task to perform; consequently it was unrealistic to train people in groups which had no task except group-introspection. For it was precisely the inter-action of the task, the group's morale and the individual's sense that needed highlighting, as I knew from my own experience as a platoon commander in a British infantry regiment in the Suez Canal Zone, and as adjutant of a Bedouin battalion in the Arab Legion.

Secondly, the Group Dynamics movement may have tended to ignore the possibility that groups which throw up their own tasks usually elect their own leaders, who remain accountable to the group. Those who are given tasks, on the other hand, have their leaders appointed 'from above', and these leaders are not wholly accountable to the group. While not denying the existence of such personality patterns, it struck me as a needless confusion to label the first category 'democratic' and the second as 'autocratic'. It could be argued that democracy cannot work without good leadership in the 'appointed' field, especially when the groups in question operate characteristically in crisis situations.

Some field research in Scotland, France, Germany and Cyprus on Sandhurst training in which I acted first as a military instructor and then as an observer convinced me that the tactical exercises where officer cadets already took roles (platoon commander, patrol leader, etc.) could become yet more valuable if the 'de-briefings' included discussion of the leadership aspect alongside the tactical lessons. But the qualities approach did not form a good enough common language for such a discussion, and there was a requirement for some preliminary introduction to the three-circle model and the widened concept of *functions* meeting the three areas of group need or leadership responsibility.

The Functional Leadership Course

Eventually by 1964 a $1\frac{1}{2}$ day's concentrated course on functional leadership was developed. In the first session the officer cadets in each company intake of 18–24 were broken up into four syndicates of 5 or 6, and asked to report back their answers to the question, What is Leadership? Their findings, written up on large sheets of newsprint, were then compared for agreements and disagreements. In this instance the small group (5 or 6) performed the essential function of stimulating thought, raising or deepening questions, challenging assumptions or cliché ideas, and arousing expectation. The plenary session, however, allowed a wider exchange. By dividing up a 90 minute session thus into both small group and plenary discussion it was possible to maximise the advantages of both and minimise their possible disadvantages.

The use of both sizes of group, 18–24 and 5–6, in a rhythmic pattern is characteristic of ACL, though of course it is widespread in other courses and conferences as well. It is especially suited to the 2- or 3-day course. In longer courses a much larger plenary group may be necessary to maintain the stock of resources necessary in the learning situation to keep up interest.

In the above description of the first session, I have outlined only one relation between the small group and plenary group. In the following sessions that relation would be changed several times. Taking the cadets out into the open, the instructor would give one of the syndicates a task to do (himself appointing the leader), and let the other three syndicates observe, giving them observation sheets with the functions of leadership required in that particular situation—planning, evaluating, encouraging, etc. So that for the first time, instead of receiving lectures on this subject, which was always unsatisfactory, the officer cadets were allowed to work it out for themselves by observing what leaders actually did in order to lead. After they have observed two or three of these syndicates in action in this way, many cadets began to grasp the functional nature of leadership. Thus, besides putting across a new concept of leadership, it was necessary to get away from monologue, from one person lecturing to an audience (which means very often that people are not having to think themselves) to a method of education whereby the cadet has to work it out for himself. This meant giving the officer cadets a chance to talk, discuss, think, test their ideas against each other, and then giving them a chance to do something, to observe and learn from action.

After this observation exercise, the officer cadets then gathered together to discuss the differences between military and industrial leadership. Here the tutor could guide the officer cadets in their syndicate and plenary discussions to appreciate the differences (as well as the similarities) between the characteristic working situations of military and civilian organisations. We also hoped that they would work out for themselves, and not need to be told, the key leadership functions required of a platoon or troop commander in the field.

This session was followed by the fourth in the evening in which the officer cadets were given a film to observe. The film which was used was *Twelve O'Clock High*, which shows first of all a leader of an American Air Force bomber group who fails because he concentrates too much on satisfying the individual needs of his followers at the expense of the other two areas, namely, the task and team maintenance. This leader is replaced by an Air Force Brigadier-General (played by Gregory Peck) after about 30 minutes of film, and although the new commanding officer does not produce perfect leadership, he does tackle it in a different way. In fact he concentrates much more on the other two areas and not so much on individual welfare.

The point of this film is that it gives officer cadets a chance to observe for themselves and pick out more evidence about leadership and its effects. The film was stopped after the first leader has been dismissed and then the cadets evaluated the first leader and then said what they would do if they were going to take over this bomber group. Then they saw the second part of the film. The film script was written by a former member of the American Eighth Air Force, and it is more akin to a documentary than to fiction.

Up to this point the course dealt mainly with leadership on active service, perhaps 90 per cent, if not more, of an officer's time is spent in less exciting fields, the barracks and the training areas. So the next session presented the cadets with a case study of a unit which has returned from overseas service with the symptoms of low morale. They were then asked to diagnose for themselves what was wrong, using the knowledge they have so far worked out for themselves on the course. Then the officer cadets suggested, in a playlet with a company commander in which they took the part of the second lieutenants, what they would do in the situation.

In the sixth session the company commander asked the officer cadets to report back on what they have learned, what more they still want to learn in this field, and how they think they can apply what they have learned already at Sandhurst and afterwards. This final session brought the course to a close, but the functional approach was picked up afterwards at frequent intervals. For example, it was used in the field training situation as a means of appraising the leadership performance of officer cadets taking the role of platoon commanders.

Industrial Applications: Size and Composition of Groups

In the trial courses at Sandhurst a plenary group of 15 working mainly in three groups of 5 members were chosen. In the first test courses in industry (Wates Ltd., 1967) it was decided to use the same number and pattern, not least because these programmes were condensed into a long working day. During 1968 the Industrial Society adopted this form of training and called it Action-Centred Leadership. Much of the effort of the Industrial Society's Leadership Department has gone into training the training managers or officers to run 'in company' ACL courses. But the Society has maintained a programme of public courses, which currently attract over 3000 managers and supervisors a year. These Industrial Society ACL courses average about 20 members, with an upper limit of 25, and are characteristically led by a single tutor.

Among the 300 or so organisations in industry, commerce and the public service who are using ACL on the in-service or in-company training programmes, similar figures have been found. In 1970 the Industrial Society published a survey (Leadership Training No. 171) based on 126 questionnaire replies from 72 organisations already involved in ACL in-company training and 54 who were about to embark upon it. The survey included the following points about numbers on courses:

The ideal number of delegates for a participatory course such as ACL is often questioned. Whatever it is should be small enough to allow a rich exchange of ideas and behaviour within the group. The Society suggests 24 as the maximum size for an ACL training group, and questions the validity of a group smaller than 12.

To discover what organisations are doing in practice, they were asked to give the average number of delegates per course. Bearing in mind non-training considerations, such as the availability of managers, the average number is likely to represent the opinion of the organisation of what is the best and most viable number for a course in practice. In fact, smaller groups dominate: two-thirds claim to keep them to 15 or below; only one-sixth 20 or above. Of course, this is influenced partly by the difficulty sometimes of collecting together a larger number in-company at the same time.

Although relatively little work has been done as yet in applying leadership training to the inter-related roles of management and unions in industry, two companies were using ACL for their shop stewards. Other groups mentioned include senior technicians, scientists, office section leaders and charge hands. Some companies found classifying jobs difficult: superintendents, for example, overlap with middle managers in one instance and with supervisors in another.

Organisations were sharply divided on the advisability of mixing levels. Of 58 companies surveyed, 31 did and 27 did not. A few of those who did specified the mixing should be diagonal to avoid a subordinate and boss on the same course. Two, however, had used the whole management team of a smaller factory as the course. Management trainees attended the supervisors course in another company, and another ran joint supervisor-shop steward ACL.

Originally the 1½ day Functional Leadership Course was designed for in-service training. Sandhurst chose to do it on the company intake basis, though the trial courses were 'stranger' groups, i.e. officer cadets from different companies who did not know each other by much more than sight. The Industrial Society's 2- and 3-day ACL courses have proved effective enough, however, and many large organisations run what are in fact 'stranger' group courses. Personally I favour the element of mixing between departments and functions, but on balance I prefer the group to be drawn from the same broad level or spectrum of management. But I have heard that experiments in mixed levels are highly effective in certain company situations.

The Limitations of ACL

Anyone as strongly associated with a form of training as I have been with Functional Leadership or ACL training gets into the habit of expounding it, extolling its merits and defending it from real or imagined criticisms. When commercial considerations crowd in even a modicum of disinterestedness is difficult to maintain. It is not for me to judge myself on that score, but I have tried to keep an open mind on the possible weaknesses of ACL as such, in contrast to the failures which come from incompetence on the trainer's part or flaws in the organisation.

Several organisations have thought that ACL does not go far enough into the social psychology of groups, and that it concentrates on the leader at the expense of the group. Certainly it would be difficult for ACL to be adapted on a wide scale to include more learning about Group Dynamics without becoming a T-Group experience, with all the implications in terms of length of course and specialist tutors (rather than general training officers or line managers) of such a move. Before moving the course in that direction on a universal basis I should want to be satisfied that I knew what more a leader (or indeed a group member) needed to understand about group dynamics than they can usefully gain through the present ACL course in terms of the universal comprehensibility of that 'more' and also its relevance to their particular jobs. Moreover, I should also like to be convinced that such extra knowledge or skill is better acquired on courses than through later experience, and that it also justifies the extra effort in terms of time and money which would be needed. Many of the proposed 'extras' I find interesting but no more. They are not relevant enough, being descriptive and open to question rather than instrumental and self-evident. These reflections are, I must confess, a general reaction to the direction which Social Psychology as a whole has largely taken since the early 1950s.

That ACL training concentrates on the leader and does less for those who are led is a more testing criticism. In the past I have resisted the idea that one can train people to become leaders solely by helping them to become good group members. So easily such a position can carry with it the assumption that leadership is the property of the group, a notion which once fathered the notion that leadership resided in the function, never in the person. So that a group function could be distinguished from a leadership function only by the fact that the latter was observed to be effective in either contributing towards the common task or building group unity. In this scheme of things a 'formal' leader (appointed or elected) was seen essentially as a safety-net, an adjunct to the group. All this accurately described the leadership of a T-Group trainer, but the uniqueness of the Group Laboratory situation was largely ignored.

Thus if one inculcates such assumptions about leadership into an organisation or group it may actually make the work of leadership more difficult. On the other hand, it could be argued that training any one to be just a leader is unrealistic because he will be always a follower or team member as well as a leader, and that it is much more logical to train him to work in a team. Against these propositions I have argued along the following two lines.

First, a really good leader paradoxically makes a good follower. It is the less able leader who often feels that he must always lead. In less good natural leaders, especially where there is a heavy if implicit reliance on the assumption that leaders are born and not made, being a good subordinate and a good 'co-ordinate' (to coin a word) do not necessarily go with leadership, as the example of Field Marshal Lord Montgomery may to some extent illustrate. The roles may mistakenly be seen as alternatives. But the best leaders evince a natural willingness to follow in situations where their knowledge and experience do not qualify them to lead; in other situations where they are qualified they can let the leadership lie latent for long periods if there are sound reasons for doing so.

Secondly, ACL training can develop a group or team member's ability to complement the work of the appointed or elected leader. In the three areas of the task, team and individual there is always more leadership work required than any one person can adequately do. But problems are created if a person with the natural ability to lead, developed through training, is given no opportunity to do so in any sphere. For this reason it is possible for any form of leadership training to arouse expectations which cannot be fulfilled in a given organisation, and produce thereby a crop of frustration.

But I can see the dangers of over-emphasising the leadership aspect at the expense of team effectiveness. They ought of course to be seen as complementary, not rivals for an either/or selection. If it had to be a choice (but it does not) I should favour the leader-centred approach because I think it more likely to produce as a by-product good followership. Yet I am equally sure that training consultants who stress the team membership aspect can also convey to their clients the distinctive importance of good leadership exercised by gifted individuals. In large-scale training it may be difficult to disentangle the assumptions about leadership which cling so obstinately to the group-centred basis of Group Dynamics in such a way that there should be no misunderstandings by the least able intellectually on the course — and they deserve close attention.

The danger of any method of training is that it bears with it latent assumptions, which — like primed time-bombs — may explode in someone else's face weeks or months after the course is over. The use of small groups in training certainly can come in this category, for any group method can be so arranged and led that the assumptions inherent in the arrangement shout louder than any verbally articulated theory or explanation of research.

Conclusion

The explosion of interest in ACL since 1967 can be explained partly by the boom in management education generally, and in particular by the popularity of 'small group activities', with a slant towards 'human relations' in content and highly participative in method. But it could also be asserted that the three-circle (or trefoil) model sums up better than any other the nature of working groups and organisations, and serves as a better introduction to leadership training than the traditional or situational theories and their modern variants. The comprehensiveness of ACL as an integrating general framework, its ability to achieve results in a relatively short time, its durability when taught by line-managers or their equivalents, and its attainment of simplicity while avoiding superficiality: all these factors make it a highly cost-effective method of leadership training.

The fact that the small group in ACL training is not used to change individuals—their attitudes or personality—has given it a clean sheet as far as nervous breakdowns or disorders are concerned. As somewhere between 50,000 and 60,000 men and women have gone through ACL training since 1964, in the armed services and industry in all parts of the world, this is a high safety record. Some may take it that this fact, coupled with the comparative brevity of the course, implies that ACL group work lacks penetrating depth. But simplicity should not be confused with superficiality, nor should it be thought that magic properties reside in mere length. Bearing in mind that ACL does not set out to use the small or plenary group to change individuals through group decisions and the like, the depth it reaches out for is more in the field of practical wisdom than personal conversion experiences.

The small group in ACL, by which I mean the 'working parties' of 5 or 6 operating in a kind of rhythm—like breathing in and out—with a parent group of 18–24, has shown itself to be a proving ground for a person's thought just as much as his feelings. And, contrary to popular ideas, the former may be more important for effective action and personal growth than the latter, for truth lasts longer than feelings. But such training needs a diet of intellectual content which is simple without being superficial and practical without being unrelated to general ideas or models. Thus it would be misleading to highlight any one element in an integrated course such as ACL, but there can be no doubt about the effectiveness of the small-plenary group system described here, or its appropriateness for adults seeking to understand and practise leadership over a relatively short length of time in the context of a particular working environment. For there is a real sense in which leadership cannot be taught—it can only be learnt.

References

1. Bird, C., *Social Psychology*, 1940.
2. Allport, G. W. and Odbert, H. S., 'Trait-names: a psycholexical study', *Psychological Monographs*, No. 211, 1936.
3. Jenkins, W. A., 'A Review of Leadership Studies with Particular Reference to Military Problems'. *Psychological Bulletin*, 1947.
4. For a discussion of these factors, see Tannenbaum, R., and Schmidt, W.H., 'How to Choose a Leadership Pattern', *Harvard Business Review* (March-April 1958); Heller, F. A., *Managerial Decision-Making: A Study of Leadership Styles and Power Sharing* (1971).

© 1979 John Adair

CHAPTER 2

Coverdale Training

BY JOHN WATERSTON

Coverdale Training is a system of planned learning experiences in small groups. They are designed to provide the means for individuals to improve their ability to get jobs done, and to improve their working relationships with others. Since its inception 15 years ago, this training has been used in a wide variety of situations: by individual managers from many different companies, by large organisations, by government departments, international agencies, sports clubs, and staff colleges. Participants have included chairmen and directors, shop floor supervisors, and all the levels of management in between.

In recent years, specialised training has been designed for social work students, youth and community workers, industry training boards, and doctoral candidates in the sciences. An experience designed to improve social relationships, for use by individuals in their personal lives, has been developed, and extensively tested by adults of widely varying age, background, and educational level.

Underlying this wide range of training experiences, for a wide variety of people with different learning needs, is a single learning method: a form of 'learning from experience' through a balanced sequence of preparation, action, and review. Similarly, there is a range of themes which underlies all forms of Coverdale Training. These themes bear on work habits, views about 'human nature', including views about the extent to which people can change themselves, and on factors affecting the working and personal relationships between people. The learning method used on Coverdale courses is designed to encourage insight, and develop understanding and skill in bringing about improvement in these distinctly human areas. The widespread belief that these human skills and qualities are unchangeable, or at least unteachable, would be challenged by the consultants engaged in Coverdale Training.

Recent experience in education, especially in Britain at the primary school level, indicates that experience-based learning is highly effective in developing skill in many school subjects previously taught by traditional methods. So it seems likely that these techniques, though still unfamiliar to the majority of adults, will be more widely accepted by succeeding generations. In future, they will certainly be applied to education and training in many fields of human activity.

Because of its potential application to other fields, it may be useful to have a description of the experiential learning method now in use by Coverdale Training consultants under relatively controlled field conditions. Because of the ineffectiveness of traditional teaching methods in enabling an individual to improve his approach to work, and his relations with others both at work and outside, it should be of interest to learn that these skills can be learnt within the context of the experiential method. Because the elements of theory presented here will be largely those which have emerged from practice, they may hope to avoid the dangers of speculation about what might be, or what ought to be.

What follows is a description and interpretation of past, present, and continuing experience. There is, therefore, much still being learnt about the application of methods already known. So it is safe to say that what is described below, in the sections on Method and Themes, represents only an interim stage of development.

1. The Early Development of the Training

Ralph Coverdale began work on what is now Coverdale Training in 1957/58, in the Steel Company of Wales. The initial research and development was in response to a need which several senior company officials saw as acute. This need was to encourage managers of the production process to accept the authority and responsibility given to them for managing men. Standing in the way of this acceptance were such difficulties as constant interruptions by telephone calls, memos, and callers, the need to meet short-term production targets, and the frequency with which managers had to 'drop everything' and concentrate their efforts on overcoming an unexpected difficulty.

These and other similar features of a process industry encouraged managers to focus on short-term tasks, dealing with each event or crisis as it arose. Under these pressures, there seemed no time to turn one's attention to the organisation of people, nor to the formulation of a long-term strategy which could give direction to present decisions.

There was another difficulty. Most managers had been promoted because of their technical expertise, from jobs in which this expertise was their chief asset. Yet after promotion, the very source of the technical expert's value to the company could, in one respect, become a liability. Managers with technical skills tended to focus their attention on the analysis of technical problems, and on attempts to find technological solutions. Yet the nature of these mens' jobs had been changed with their promotion from technical experts to managers. Formerly, their work had been to use their own specialised knowledge and skill; it was now to manage other specialists, whose technical expertise required co-ordination. Yet nothing in their past experience had prepared them for this change.

The money available for training at that time was being used to send managers to universities, management colleges, and technical institutes to gain knowledge about management techniques. But the relating of theory to practice back at work was not taking place on a satisfactory scale. What 'ought to be' in one theoretical set of circumstances was often found to be unrelated or inappropriate to the circumstances which actually prevailed back at work. In addition, many managers returned from courses without the skill to use their new knowledge in implementing constructive changes.

Ralph Coverdale invited Bernard Babington Smith, who had been his tutor at Oxford, to join in evolving and testing methods to help managers acquire skill in dealing with human, interactive situations. The first course was run in 1959 with 20 participants. It lasted a fortnight and was fully residential, thereby enabling an intensive programme to be conducted without outside distractions. It was immediately apparent that the small group work was making a tremendous impact on the participants.

The early course invited the active participation of managers attending them: they took part in carrying out short jobs or 'tasks' in collaboration with others, learning from this first-hand experience how to work more effectively. They participated in the evaluation of their own experience and then took steps to improve their performance. In so doing, the course members made an important contribution to the evolution of the training, since some of the techniques they tried and found successful were incorporated into later designs. This principle, of starting with an open mind and evolving a theory from direct personal and collective experience, has been a fundamental precept throughout the development of Coverdale Training. Its evolution has been through a series of discoveries by staff and course members alike, working together in the face of real human and management difficulties.

Ralph Coverdale's primary concern was that whatever was learnt in training should be applied back at work. If the managers who attended these courses were seen to be more effective in their working relationships and in their ability to manage, then the training could be judged useful to industry. The outcome of learning amongst managers must be evident in what they do, not only in what they know.

2. Early Findings

From the early 2-week courses onwards, Coverdale and his colleagues developed firmer views about how future training should be structured. These views have remained as guidelines for course design to the present time.

(i) Individuals in groups must have opportunities for physical activity, in order to release the mental stress which can be the by-product of intensive verbal efforts to clarify meanings and to improve co-operation. To provide these opportunities, tasks should be designed which require some or all the group members to leave the working room and venture outside: to collect information or materials, report results to the staff, seek co-operation from other working groups, and the like.

(ii) Self-confidence and mutual trust in others must be built up in each course member. It is seldom present in groups of individuals coming together for the first time, but its development can be encouraged by the design of the course, and by the supportive behaviour of the staff. They must nurture the self-confidence which grows with achievement during the course. Only when it is firmly established can there follow a growing confidence in others.

Coverdale saw the building up of confidence, in the light of successful experience, as essential to the learning aims of management training. When confidence was present, course members were willing to face directly the human issues which arose, and deal with them constructively. When confidence was absent, individuals reverted to 'putting up a good front', and learning ceased.

As a means of fostering confidence, the training staff undertook to make no reports on the performance of individual course members to the organisations which sponsored them. During the course itself, when working groups reported to each other, specific events were described but names were not mentioned. Thus, knowledge of 'who did what, in a syndicate was limited to those who had shared in the experience at first hand. This procedure preserved the growing confidence between syndicate members, and thereby encouraged them to take the risk of trying out new and unfamiliar practices to improve co-operation.

(iii) Course members should be encouraged to observe consciously what was happening in their syndicates. This would enable them to provide their colleagues with observers' reports in detail, and with accuracy, so that the syndicate members could act upon them.

It became increasingly clear that observation was a fundamental management skill, a necessary prerequisite to improving a manager's ability to behave constructively in any working group. The course design must, therefore, enable every course member to practise the skill of observation. Initially, this could best be achieved by giving each member of a syndicate, in turn, the opportunity to sit back from the task which the other members in his syndicate were carrying out. This would allow the observing member to see the total situation from an objective point of view, noting what actions people took and what effects these actions had.

By the end of the course, each individual should have had sufficient practice in observation to enable him to become a skilled observer whilst doing tasks himself. This was the ideal desired on their return to ordinary work.

(iv) The protracted analysis of difficulties should not be allowed to drive a group into frustration, depression, and loss of confidence. In fact, it should not be allowed at all until a group and its members have developed the capacity and skill to implement improvements. This is not to say that drawing attention to difficulties is in itself harmful; on the contrary, awareness that a problem existed was seen to provide a powerful incentive to seek ways of overcoming it. A group which was already confident in its ability to carry out tasks successfully could then apply and modify its successful practices to overcome difficulties. Thus the focus of attention on a course should initially be on success, and the causes of success. After a body of practices had been tried and found successful, a syndicate could face its problems with confidence and deal with them constructively.

(v) After mutual trust and confidence is established within a syndicate, exercises should be introduced to develop each individual's skill in recognising strengths and abilities in himself and in others. It was evident that people saw only too readily what was wrong with things and with the people round them. Obstacles and weaknesses were pointed out in gruesome detail; satisfying results were often dismissed with a 'Well, that wasn't bad. But let's examine where we went wrong'. If individuals could identify specific abilities in their colleagues, particularly skills in fostering co-operation, the syndicates could turn these skills to account for the benefit of all. If an individual manager could apply this same practice to his ordinary work, the skills and human strengths of his boss, his colleagues and subordinates could be better utilised to the benefit of the organisation, while meeting every person's need to be recognised for what he can do well.

The application of these guidelines to their course designs led Ralph Coverdale and Bernard Babington Smith to conclude that the training was now much better than traditional teaching in improving skill in co-operation. Design development continued at Esso Petroleum Company Limited, which Ralph Coverdale joined in 1961 as Head of Management Studies. One of the first innovations at Esso was the halving of the length of the basic course. Originally lasting a fortnight, it was redesigned to take only 5 days. Yet most of the original themes were still explored by course members, for a time sufficient to enable them to begin to develop skill in their use.

In addition, new themes were included: thinking in terms of purpose, and setting aims for tasks to be carried out; and deliberately planning to improve the way people work together, in the light of observation.

These developments formed the basis of what is now Coverdale Training, and were tested within Esso on a very large scale. It is convenient, therefore, to end our account of the training's early development here, and incorporate the fruits of the research and testing at Esso in the sections on the Method and the Themes of Coverdale Training.

3. Features of the Method

(i) LEARNING FROM EXPERIENCE

The principle which characterises all Coverdale courses is that participants shall learn as much as possible from first-hand experience, gained through taking action to get things done. In Coverdale Training, this action generally occurs in the carrying out of short, achievable tasks by small working groups. The content and emphasis of Coverdale courses vary widely, since they are designed to meet varying requirements and objectives; the learning method, however, remains constant.

For many companies, the first contact with Coverdale Training occurs when several key managers attend Coverdale Preparatory (Part I) Conferences. At the start of many of these conferences, syndicate members are asked to recall successful practices they have used in the past, when working with other people. These then become the basis for the operation of the syndicate during its first task. Later, after reviewing what happened, changes are made and new plans laid in the light of the effects of the practices used.

As the course progresses, syndicate members continue to try out practices which they believe will improve their ability to co-operate to get things done. Each time, they examine what happened as a result of their actions. They then make proposals which build on the successes of the past, and incorporate them in their plans for working together effectively in future. They try out these plans in doing another task, and review again, thereby developing the habit of planning for continuous improvement.

New practices which work in specific situations are exchanged with members of other syndicates, who can then try them out. As a result, a body of successful principles and practices begins to build up on every Coverdale course. Each course member knows from personal experience that these practices *work*. This experience gives a manager the confidence to apply the practices developed and used on the course to his job, where the risks are greater. With repeated use, in a variety of circumstances, some practices are seen to have a generally beneficial effect on the working relationships between people. It is this progressive application from the course to the work environment which Coverdale Training is designed to foster.

The continuous cycle described above is one of *preparation, action*, and *reviewing to improve* in the next period of action. Its incorporation into the course design is one way of enabling managers to discover that they can constructively control their environment. The systematic use of this cycle ensures that course members will have experiences from which they can learn.

There are other aspects of design which also help to create an environment conducive to learning from experience, an environment which encourages people to take the risks inevitably associated with making discoveries and learning from them.

(ii) THE STRUCTURE AND MEMBERSHIP OF COURSES

Most Coverdale Training courses last for 5 days and are residential. They are conducted away from the place of work, usually in a hotel, so that the participants may enjoy a low-risk environment in which they can feel free to try out new ways of overcoming difficulties. Most managers are reluctant to risk using untested methods in the work situation; not only is their performance subject to constant evaluation by superiors and subordinates, but the consequences of wasting valuable financial, material, and human resources can be severe. During Coverdale courses, therefore, the tasks which syndicates are invited to carry out use inexpensive materials, and have consequences which mainly affect the working relationships within the syndicates themselves. Coverdale consultants continue the practice of treating the performance of individuals on courses as confidential. Thus the course design reduces some of the risks which confront most managers at work, making it easier for them to learn from their course experiences.

The ideal size for most Coverdale Training courses is between 18 and 28 members, working in three or four syndicates of 6 or 7 members each. Within these limits, there is ample time for exchanges of information between syndicates when the whole course meets together. It is also possible for a Course Director to readily co-ordinate the work of up to four syndicates.

(iii) THE USE OF TASKS

The rationale for using the task, rather than the case study or discussion as the basis of Coverdale Training courses, has been set out in a previously published article. As stated there, tasks are used for four main reasons:

First, managers can never know how well they have planned and prepared to do something, unless they actually test their plans by carrying them out. This gives them experience, which they can then review in order to learn how to make better preparations next time.

Second, the purpose of management—to get things done—is kept to the fore. Managers in training are not allowed to stroll through a shadow-land of hypothesis, but are encouraged to find a realistic balance between thinking and doing.

Third, the human and emotional issues which arise when people do things together—which is the work situation—are different from those which arise when people merely talk together about what they might do in hypothetical circumstances.

Fourth, the experience of having to change assumptions gives rise to tensions and frustrations. Working at practical tasks provides a safety valve, a means of dispersing tensions.[1]

While the central requirement at work is to get tasks done, during a Coverdale course tasks are used as vehicles for learning how to co-operate in a wide variety of situations similar to those at work. Each task is designed to highlight particular human issues which arise in doing jobs at work. In this way, course members can gain specific skills in overcoming specific human difficulties.

One difficulty which most managers have encountered, for example, arises from receiving an instruction from the boss which is phrased in very general terms. One hardy perennial in many organisations is the request to 'Improve the efficiency of your department'. Before this request can be tackled or delegated with some certainty that a satisfactory result will be achieved, an instruction like this must be made more specific. There are a number of ways in which this can be done. One relevant line of questioning is this: Why has the instruction been given? What purposes are the results asked for intended to serve? Finding answers to these questions may help those who carry out the request to do so in the spirit in which it was given, producing the desired result. They will often be able to specify what has to be done after they know the purpose of doing the job.

To give course members practice in thinking in terms of purpose, for example, one task instruction which might be given during a course could be, 'Report on safety hazards in the vicinity'. A syndicate of 6 or 7 members would be given 1 hour to carry out this instruction. Afterwards, half an hour would be scheduled for a systematic review of what happened. What issues arose? How were they dealt with? What practices were successfully used and should be repeated? What difficulties were encountered and still remain to be overcome? How could they be overcome if they arose again? Questions such as these are likely to be considered during the syndicate's review of the task and the way they tackled it.

There are hundreds of tasks designed to give participants practice in dealing with a wide range of human issues. There are tasks to develop skill in the allocation of limited resources, and tasks which raise the issue of gaining others' commitment to personal learning aims for the week. Some tasks require extensive planning before action can be initiated; others lend themselves to an early period of experimentation to collect information. There are tasks which encourage the use of foresight to envisage what the end product might look like, creative, abstract tasks, and tasks which invite attention to detail.

All the tasks in Coverdale courses have this in common: they require people to work together to carry them out. Different ways of working together (for example, different styles of leadership or co-ordination) may be most effective for different sorts of tasks. The consideration of which practices are appropriate to a given type of task is a major issue in the syndicate reviews following each period of activity.

We have noted above that most Coverdale tasks are short and technically relatively simple, by comparison with those managers typically face at work. Tasks which meet both these criteria allow course members to focus their attention on how they are working together, rather than on the technicalities of the job in hand. All the tasks used on Coverdale courses for managers are related to jobs at work, in that the same or similar human issues arise in both. On the course, as at work, these issues need to be resolved constructively.

(iv) THE SYNDICATE COACH

Working with each syndicate during many Coverdale courses is a Coverdale consultant, serving the syndicate as a 'coach'. He or she is called a 'coach' because their job is similar to that of any team coach: to encourage and support the team, observe how they work together, point out successful practices worth repeating and difficulties to be overcome, and make constructive suggestions for improvement.

Coaches need to be skilled observers, and a coach's first aim is to develop the skill of observation in each member of his syndicate. To this end, he intervenes in the early stages of a course to set an example of accurate and specific observation. Thereafter, as the syndicate members notice more things themselves, the coach will draw their attention to significant occurrences when these are overlooked.

During most of the time the syndicate is working on tasks, the coach sits to one side, noting what happens. When he intervenes it will often be to ask a question, or to make observations, rather than to interpret what is happening. The effect of a well-phrased and well-timed observation or question from the coach is often to make the group stop what it is doing, and think. A coach might say, for example, 'Bill hasn't said anything during this task', or ask, 'What is the risk of actually trying out that idea?', or, 'Have you finished the job to your satisfaction?'. In these examples, the syndicate are, by implication, being asked to consider the issue raised by their coach, draw their own conclusions, and act on them. Coaches often judge it better not to intervene during a task, but to draw the attention of the syndicate to some issue during the review that follows each task.

If a coach makes interpretations before the task is completed, the effect can be unconstructive. Let us say that a coach observes that Bill has kept silent, and interprets this observation in the comment, 'Bill is unwilling to express his opinions'. It is easy to see that this could be the first shot in a battle of words and wills. Is the interpretation right or wrong? To take another example, suppose a coach interprets a syndicate's more than generous allowance of time to their planning for a simple task by saying, 'You seem to be trying to avoid getting into action'. He might well be met with the retort, 'We were just about to!' To get into situations such as these, in which one side 'wins' and the other 'loses', diverts attention from the experience itself,. and therefore from the course members' likelihood of learning from it.

The coach helps a syndicate to discover general principles underlying their experiences on the course, and so to see applications to situations back at work. He also draws their attention to similarities between the difficulties in achieving co-operation which they are now overcoming on the course, and those which exist in their everyday jobs. This is a vital part of the coach's function, for many course members find it difficult to make the leap from abstract principles to real practice, and from the course environment to that at work.

Many coaches consistently refrain from making comments evaluating the worth of individuals' actions. Questions about whether a given course of action is 'right' or 'wrong', 'good' or 'bad', are often asked of coaches, and just as often thrown back on the syndicate members who have experienced this course of action, and its consequences. This is because it is one of the coach's aims to develop the ability of every syndicate member to evaluate accurately the effects of his own and others' actions on a working group. To this end, the coach insists that syndicate members draw their own conclusions, and put these to the test by acting on them in the next task.

A coach's insistence on self-evaluation is sometimes misunderstood. Most managers are accustomed to being told how they are doing by someone else, often someone with authority over their future prospects. A coach's response to a request for evaluation — 'Well, what effect do *you* think your plans had?' — is sometimes mistaken for evasiveness. Yet the coach has no option but to persevere in his refusal to evaluate, explaining why, until individuals have sufficient confidence first to venture their own judgements, and then, through experience, to rely on them.

This is not to say, of course, that the coach does not support his syndicate in their efforts. Support is provided, especially initially, by the coach's factual and specific observations on the successes of the team. He gives credit where it is due: 'It was after Bill clarified the purpose of this task that ideas about how to do the job were produced'. The coach also tries to ensure that in review the syndicate considers its successful practices, and builds on these in their subsequent plans and actions.

Finally, on many Coverdale courses it is the coach who is the direct link between the individual and the course. He administers the programme of work for his syndicate and may vary it, in consultation with the Course Director, to suit their special interests. He works with individuals who have special needs or difficulties to overcome, either on the course or back at work. At good deal of individual attention is made possible by having one skilled coach for each syndicate of six or seven, and by making use of the 'free' time during residential courses.

The work of the coach is demanding and arduous, requiring continuous concentration, a high degree of skill, courage and integrity.

4. Training Themes

During every Coverdale course, many practices and principles to foster cooperation are touched upon, and some are explored in considerable depth. In order to help course members to use them during their course, and to recall them afterwards, these practices and principles have been grouped together under seven training themes. These themes are described below. They comprise the content of a Coverdale course, studied by the method of learning from planned experiences.

(i) EVOLVING AIMS

During a course, aims are evolved both by individuals and by syndicates. Course members practice describing what has to be achieved, and for what purpose. Coaches encourage them to make explicit what the results of a given task can be used for, and, in addition, which of their learning aims they will work towards in carrying out that task.

In a complex, abstract task with a useful end result, syndicates are asked to create a synthesis of the aims of its individual members (*not* a compromise between them). If it can be achieved, this synthesis enables each syndicate member to contribute constructively towards both his own and others' aims, with the result that commitment to the group's work is established. Creating a synthesis of aims does not imply conformity, but rather a voluntary acceptance of—and commitment to—mutually agreed purposes which everyone understands.

Participants practice clarifying their own and others' understanding of the aims they are pursuing. This involves stating aims specifically, so that people can see what action is required to achieve them. It also involves stating aims unambiguously, so that group members do not waste effort and become frustrated by unintentionally working towards different ends.

Coaches encourage participants to focus on particular objectives within the context of wider and longer-term aims, so that immediate action can be directed towards their achievement. Step by step, as short-term objectives are achieved, confidence grows. Eventually, what at first appeared to be too complex or too high an aspiration 'even to think about' becomes achievable, by the completion of the last of a series of manageable steps.

With increasing precision, syndicate members try to set measures by which they can judge for themselves their progress towards the specific aims of each task, and their learning aims for the week. Answering certain questions can help in the setting of these measures of progress towards aims: 'How will we know when we have completed the job to our own satisfaction?', 'How can we determine in advance whether our results will be acceptable to those for whom they are intended?', 'What specific things should be happening in our syndicate when (for instance) everyone is listening better?'.

(ii) A SYSTEMATIC APPROACH TO GETTING THINGS DONE

This is an elaboration of the cycle of preparation, action, and reviewing to improve. It is a progression through a series of stages, leading to the achievement of aims. Its balanced sequence of thought and action provides the framework for learning from experience in Coverdale Training.

A Systematic Approach to Getting Things Done is but a method; the ends to which this method is directed must be established before the method itself can be effectively used. Thus the first step, before using A Systematic Approach in a group, is for those who will do the work to arrive at a commonly understood and shared set of *aims*.

They can then collect *information* relevant to the achievement of these aims.

In the light of the information, one or more members of the group come to see *what has to be done* in order to work towards the achievement of the group's aims.

By envisaging what the results of this work will produce, the group can set itself *measures for judging success* in completing what has to be done.

Then, who does what, when, and how can be specified in a *plan* for action to achieve the agreed aims.

With the plan commonly understood and accepted, and its relevance to the aims checked, the members of the working group can take the risk of going into *action* to carry out the plan.

After the action is completed, the group can *review* what happened in the light of their experience, *and plan to improve* in future.

The review is typically divided into two parts: the review of the task just completed, and a review of the group's progress towards its immediate or longer-term learning aims.

In the review of the task, the Systematic Approach cycle begins again. Information is collected about the results of the action the syndicate has just taken. This information about what has been achieved is evaluated, using the measures for judging success which were previously set. If these measures are not yet met, and there is more that has to be done, a new plan can be made and another stage of action completed to carry it out. Then, again, the results can be assessed against the measures set.

In the syndicate's review of progress towards its learning aims, the Systematic Approach cycle is again repeated. In this case, the syndicate's learning aims, and the information relevant to them are likely to be more complex than the aims and information applicable to any task.

A Systematic Approach to Getting Things Done is used on Coverdale courses both by individuals working alone and by working groups. For individuals it serves as an effective problem-solving tool. In groups, its use is designed to establish a commonly understood and agreed procedure for working through any task. As such, it helps to overcome a common difficulty experienced by people trying to work together. The 'problem' is that each person approaches the same kind of work in a different way. One may query the purpose it is intended to serve, another looks round to see what resources are available, and what relevant facts are already known, while another is adept at dividing up the elements of the job amongst those present. And there is usually at least one man eager to leap into action at once: 'Let's just get on and *do* it!'

In a group which has agreed to use A Systematic Approach, each individual can see the stages at which his contributions can be used immediately by the group in their progress through a task. Questions about the purpose of the task need to be settled before what has to be done becomes clear, and plans can be made. These plans need to take account of the relevant information, so planning must be deferred until information is known. In this way, a working group can use the progression through A Systematic Approach, from aims to action, as a framework for co-operation.

Even when only one person in a working group is aware of the potential benefits of using A Systematic Approach to Getting Things Done, he can personally time his contributions so that they can be immediately built upon by others in his group. If he believes that the aims of a job or a meeting are being lost sight of, that insufficient weight is being given to a stage of A Systematic Approach, or that these stages are being tackled in an order which is less than ideal, his experience on the course enables him to make constructive suggestions to his colleages at work.

Participants on Coverdale courses devote considerable time and effort to learning how to use A Systematic Approach *flexibly*, on a variety of different tasks. Used rigidly, as a mechanism, it is no more than a dangerous substitute for thought. Where information must be evaluated, and actions have consequences, no method can be used without continually judging its appropriateness.

A majority of past course members say, when asked, that this is the training theme that they have used most widely in their work.

(iii) OBSERVATION

From the first task on a Coverdale course, the staff encourage course members to expand their awareness of what is happening to encompass the whole situation. There is the task itself, the action being taken to carry out the task, the organisation of the group taking the action, its procedures and practices. There are the emotional aspects of the group: the ways its members interact, the feelings of individuals towards one another and towards the organisation, procedures, and aims of the group, and the evaluative judgements members make about the attributes, reliability, and integrity of their colleagues. To see all these aspects of the situation whilst sitting back from the task as an observing member requires considerable skill. It also requires an interest in the distinctively human aspects of getting things done. This grows as course members come to realise how close is the link between effective human interaction and high quality results.

More demanding than the role of the observing member on the course is that of the manager at work: to observe the work environment in detail *whilst* doing tasks himself. Only a start is made in developing this skill in course members during a first 5-day experience. During this time, those who recognise the importance of observation to a manager of men begin to develop this skill. They carry forward observations made in the review stage of A Systematic Approach into proposals for improvement; this enables them to test the accuracy and depth of their observations by their consequences in action. They see that their comments on what they have observed have an effect on their colleagues' ability to co-operate. This in turn creates the confidence and interest necessary to continue to practise observing back at work, even under pressure of doing tasks themselves.

As the course progresses, the Coverdale staff encourage course members to *use* their observations as *information*, in A Systematic Approach to improving co-operation.

(iv) PLANNING CO-OPERATION TO MUTUAL BENEFIT

We have noted some of the ways in which syndicate members practise using A Systematic Approach to plan improvements to the way they work together. In addition, course members are offered procedures for using the skills and strengths of their colleagues to the benefit of all. The staff's aim is to enable each syndicate to make the most of individual differences in thinking styles and abilities, particularly abilities which facilitate co-operation between people. These include skills in supporting others' ideas, clarifying, getting into action, making constructive suggestions, and the like. What the Coverdale staff try to foster in this area is just the opposite of conformity. A group which uses the different personalities and skills of its members to the full can achieve far more than any individual, and more than any group whose members must conform to a single norm.

(v) SKILL RECOGNITION

Before the skills, strengths, and qualities of syndicate members can be used by others in the group, they must be recognised. Since Coverdale courses are task-centred, individual's skills begin to emerge from the very first. As different tasks are carried out, so the variety of skills of syndicate members emerge and are recognised. They can then be deliberately used by the group when they are most appropriate.

One of the most important tasks of most managers is to perceive the potential strengths and skills in their subordinates, and to support these to the benefit of the individual and the organisation. During Coverdale courses, therefore, the focus is on perceiving what people can do well, and establishing the conditions which will enable them to use their abilities still better. After this has openly been done, it is then appropriate to examine those areas in which individuals could do better, and possibly to do this openly as well. When people know they are recognised for what they can do well, they have the confidence essential to the constructive consideration of areas in which they are less competent. In the knowledge of what they *can* do, moreover, lie potential alternatives to unsatisfactory practices.

(vi) LISTENING AND PROPOSING

As course members work together on tasks, the need to listen to each other soon becomes apparent. The first comment often comes from an observing member, amazed that anything was accomplished in the chaos of crosstalk that filled the room. In the review, it emerges that ideas were lost, directions had to be repeated several times, and the misunderstandings were rife. In response to this information, syndicates often make plans to ensure that each member's comments are heard and noted before others put forward their ideas, and that there is a procedure for ensuring that everyone who wishes to contribute is called upon. Freed from the need to fight to get a word in edgeways, syndicate members are free to listen to their colleagues.

(vii) AUTHORITY

In most organisations, the amount of authority a manager has over policy decisions and resources depends on his position in the organisation's management hierarchy. The executives at the top of the hierarchy have most authority over their organisation's aims and the distribution of its human and material resources. The further down the hierarchy a manager is, the less of this sort of authority he has.

In contrast, a manager's authority to improve co-operation between himself and those he works with does *not* depend on his position in the organisational hierarchy. Everyone in an organisation, from managing director to secretary, has *equal* authority to improve the way he works with others. With every exercise of this sort of authority, a manager influences the extent to which others are willing to co-operate with him.

On Coverdale courses, attention is focused on this distinction between the authority over policy and the distribution of resources and the authority to improve co-operation. The Coverdale staff put forward the view that no chairman or leader has the power to enforce co-operation in a group. If it exists, it has been brought about through the active efforts of those who are working together. These efforts necessarily involve others besides the leader in taking the initiative to suggest practices for improving co-operation, and in using them.

It is, of course, easy enough to say that each member of a group *can* take upon himself the authority for improving the ability of all to work together. He is only likely to do so, however, if he knows what to do, and has practised doing it where the risks were low. This is what Coverdale Training is designed to allow. Techniques for improving work with others are presented and discovered, then repeatedly practised until skill in their use begins to develop. When an individual has the capacity to improve co-operation to the benefit of all, he is ready to accept the authority for doing so.

5. The Range of Courses

The Coverdale Organisation run two distinct sorts of courses. There are 'public' courses, designed for managers from a wide variety of different organisations, and touching on all the training themes. There are also 'in-company' courses, designed for specific organisations. Here it is possible to give the course members the opportunity to concentrate their attention on those themes most relevant to their organisation's needs and objectives. These are established in advance insofar as possible, by interviews with managers at all levels. Of particular interest for the purpose of course design is any marked contrast which may exist between past practices, organisational structure, and policy, and that which now obtains or is planned for the future.

Working closely with a number of organisations, Coverdale consultants have designed comprehensive organisation development strategies to meet particular needs. These strategies may employ any or all of the three basic courses described below, in addition to pre-course interviews and extensive follow-through consultancy on the work site. Coverdale consulting services are not discussed here, since they are not small group learning experiences. They are, however, an integral part of any effective organisation development programme. An increasing number of Coverdale courses are now linked to a specified period of follow-through consultancy, aimed at encouraging the application of the training themes to specific work problems.

(i) THE PREPARATORY CONFERENCE (PART I)

The purpose of these courses, whether 'public' or 'in-company', is to provide a learning experience in which delegates will discover and practise methods for continuous self-improvement, and will develop skills useful in managing other people. Though all seven training themes are generally touched on, several are likely to be explored in depth. Three of these are certain to be A Systematic Approach to Getting Things Done, Skill Recognition, and Evolving Aims.

In addition, participants are encouraged from the start to engage in Planning Co-operation to Mutual Benefit, by applying A Systematic Approach to observations of how syndicate members worked together.

Each course member works in one syndicate of 6 or 7 for the full 5 days of this residential course, with a few exceptions. These occur when new groupings are formed to facilitate the exchange of information between syndicates, and when members with similar jobs work together to plan how to apply the training to their work.

(ii) THE APPLICATION CONFERENCE (PART II)

Its purpose is to enable delegates to discover ways of operating effectively in a variety of teams, and to develop their skill in leadership. In addition, the Application Conference provides a further opportunity to develop those skills practised during the Preparatory Conference.

In order that they can make the best use of this opportunity, delegates are recommended to spend from 3 to 6 months back at work, using the plans made during their Part I course. They then bring to the Part II an understanding of *how* the discoveries of the Part I can be applied to their own practical needs at work.

The most distinctive feature of the Application Conference is that delegates are members of at least three different groups during the week. One set of syndicates is subdivided into steering and working parties in which some course members make plans to be acted upon when others join them. Another set of syndicates meets periodically throughout the week, engaged on a longer-term research, development, and production project. Before the production phase of their work, a small Management Group is formed to direct their activities. One of the main challenges facing the Management Group is to generate the commitment of the other course members to the decisions and plans which the Group will ask them to carry out. The third syndicate of which each delegate is a member is his 'base' group. Its principal functions are to collect and disseminate information about successful practices in co-operating with others, and to suggest ways in which the other syndicates can improve their ability to achieve their aims.

As can be seen from this description, the theme of Authority is prominent in the Application Conference. Both the authority over policy and resources and the authority to improve co-operation are explored in considerable depth.

(iii) THE PART III CONFERENCE

At present, a limited number of these courses are held each year. They vary in content depending on the needs of the participants. Part III Conferences have been designed for Directors and General Managers, who are especially concerned with organisation development. They give the course members opportunities to gain skill in coaching their fellow participants, an activity which Ralph Coverdale regarded as similar in many respects to good management practice in an organisation.

(iv) OTHER SCHEDULED COURSES

These are all designed to enable participants to learn from first-hand experience. They include:

One-day Application Seminars, designed to reinforce the ability of ex-delegates to apply Coverdale Training themes to their specific needs at work.

The Coverdale Sales Programme, designed to enable salesmen and managers concerned with marketing to increase their skill in presenting their product or service to the public.

Supervising for Results, to help supervisors become more skilled at managing others and solving problems at work.

Other courses are likely to be introduced as Coverdale methods of learning from experience are applied to meet other needs.

6. Evaluating the Training

(i) EVALUATION BASED ON A DESCRIPTION OF THE TRAINING

In this chapter I have tried to give a reasonably clear description of a form of small group training dealing systematically with highly complex human skills. I have tried also to describe the learning method and themes of Coverdale Training so as to show their consistency with the training's aims. There are at least three good reasons, however, against basing an evaluation of Coverdale Training on what is written here.

First, the emphasis placed on aspects of the development, method, and themes of the training must inevitably be a personal one. In a description written by another Coverdale consultant, one would see Coverdale Training from a different viewpoint, based on different experience. Our organisation is a company of individualists, each with his or her own interest in applying the fundamentals of Coverdale Training to particular fields. In this diversity is strength, since there is a constant stream of new developments from many consultants, working in different areas, and using different techniques and tasks to achieve a common end: the development of skill in the training themes.

Second, since the Coverdale learning method is based on the experience of course members, each Coverdale course is unique in its own right. Any one course is likely to be very closely related to the description given here in some respects, less closely in others. A preliminary assessment of Coverdale Training's suitability to a particular need *could* be made from a written statement such as this, but it is the courses themselves, rather than statements, which affect people's skill in co-operation. Evaluations of effectiveness must be evaluations of the effects of particular courses on particular individuals.

Third, it is comparatively easy to write a description of Coverdale Training in which the constituent parts are consistent one with another. It is very much harder to run a course with complete consistency. A perfect harmony between the training's aims and the method used to attain them, between the course design and the interventions of coaches, between the skill we try to develop and that which does in fact develop—this harmony is an ideal often approached but seldom achieved to our complete satisfaction. Coverdale consultants *know* a good deal about the design of courses which will promote learning, about giving instructions which will be interpreted as they were intended to be, and about the different sorts of comments which enable a syndicate at work to work better. But *applying* this knowledge in a difficult and perhaps unique situation is not easy, and our ability to do so, like that of our course members, is improvable.

(ii) EVALUATION BASED ON THE EFFECTS OF THE TRAINING

A number of different organisations have evaluated the effects of Coverdale Training, for different purposes and under widely varying conditions. Our own Company initiates many evaluations of the impact of our courses on the work of ex-delegates. Often, our purpose in doing this is to ensure a continuing check on the appropriateness of particular courses to the requirements they are designed to meet.

Some evaluative surveys are conducted by or for the organisations using Coverdale Training, to help them judge whether an initial investment in training is worth continuing, or perhaps extending more widely.

Below are extracts from some of the most recent evaluative studies of Coverdale Training courses and projects. In several examples, statements have been paraphrased to avoid explicit reference to particular individuals or organisations, where this has been requested.

(a) Courses for the Food and Agriculture Organisation of the United Nations

After a series of three pilot Preparatory (Part I) Courses, held in Italy for F.A.O., Coverdale Training Limited sought to determine whether the training was being applied and, if so, how. In addition, we wished to assess what future training and follow-through could most effectively build on what had already been achieved. To these ends, the Coverdale consultants who had directed and coached on the pilot courses gathered examples of applications from the course delegates. One example is as follows:

On a project embarked on since his Coverdale course, one official reports that he has spent much more time and effort than previously in informing everybody involved and in listening to their views. He now sees this as an essential and continuing part of his work. He says, 'Formerly I would have been somewhat impatient with this and half-consider it an imposition. I was anxious to get down to the "real" work, but now I realise this *is* half the managerial work, and am allowing time for it in my schedules.'[2]

(b) A course for the Department of Employment

The Department's computer team, composed mainly of computer programmers and systems analysts, was in some difficulty in 1971. Senior members of the team believed that: 'A failure on the part of members of the DE team to acquire the skills which would enable them to work together with greater efficiency had led to a number of problems. Deadlines were rarely met, objectives were not always clearly understood by all concerned and there was a tendency for Systems Analysts and Programmers to blame each other when things went wrong. The meeting agreed that Coverdale Training seemed well-suited to the Department's needs.'[3]

A selected sample from the computer team attended a Coverdale Preparatory (Part I) Course, monitored by members of the Civil Service Department Behavioural Sciences Research Division. Afterwards, a 26-page report evaluating the effectiveness of the course was prepared by Mr. Neil Ferguson of the BSRD. In the Summary which prefaces his report, Ferguson states that:

The main findings are that a Coverdale Training course had the following effects:

(1) Trainees showed a markedly improved tendency to be in possession of the same agreed facts at the end of a small working group session in which a number of ideas and decisions were communicated.

(2) Trainees felt that they had a more positive attitude towards their work.

(3) Trainees were much more confident of their ability to handle small group meetings.

(4) Trainees were more convinced of the need to check for understanding when issuing instructions.

(5) After the training course, Coverdale Trainees perceived consultation with colleagues at work as a more important activity than they had before the course.

(6) Systems analysts' and programmers' co-operation was seen as greatly improved following training.

(7) There was some evidence to show that hostility between systems analysts and programmers was reduced after training.

(8) Coverdale Training had no significant effect on job satisfaction.

(9) Coverdale Trainees in a small working group tended to spend more time concentrating on aspects of procedure and made fewer proposals which could be used to solve the problem.

The problems which were identified were not all amenable to the effects of training but the Coverdale approach did seem to have relevance to some of the computer team's difficulties.[4]

(c) A training programme for a large international company

In 1970–71, a series of eight 1-week residential Preparatory (Part I) Courses was held at one of this Company's Works. All day and shift supervisors and managers, some members of the clerical staff, and a few other personnel attended these courses: a total of 174 employees. In addition, 14 senior managers and heads of departments attended Coverdale Public Preparatory Courses. This training programme was initiated following a statement by Senior Management that what was particularly needed was an improvement 'with respect to the quality of decisions, team work, development of subordinates and solving organisational problems'.[5] In each of these areas, more specific objectives were set.

At the end of the training period of 11 months, a report was produced by Senior Management on the general effectiveness of the Coverdale Preparatory Course in meeting their objectives. Below are three excerpts from a digest of this report.

Regarding *Accident Prevention*, the report . . . said that 66% of the improvement that had occurred between 1969 and 1970 was due to Works activity. It added that the principles used had largely depended on Coverdale Training. An important feature was the setting of numerical targets for each plant or group . . . The report found 'an increase in candour due to a jointly defined objective on dangerous occurrence and accident investigations: "To prevent recurrence",' adding that many incidents which might in the past have been concealed were voluntarily and formally reported.[6] Ten examples were cited of savings achieved or promised as a result of Coverdale-inspired approaches to problems. (The Coverdale Systematic Approach was twice specifically mentioned.) . . . The lower limit [of cost savings] represented an annual saving equivalent to the total cost of the [training] programme; the upper limit was three times as great.[7]

On *Inter-Group Collaboration*, the report found 'significant improvement'. It acknowledged that such collaboration was fostered by Coverdale Training, with its emphasis on the establishment of a mutually acceptable objective which encouraged co-operation, and on the need to recognise and use the skills and expertise of individuals. Instances of improvement were quoted: the settlement of differences between production and engineering staff by frank exposure and discussion of unsatisfactory situations; the establishment of working parties to discuss vexed problems of communications, stores, and transport, and improve efficiency in specific areas, modifications on plants to produce saving on maintenance effected through joint meetings of production-maintenance teams ('making conscious and deliberate use of Coverdale Training methods').[8]

(d) A training and consultancy project for a national production and distribution company

At the end of a pilot project including specialised Coverdale courses, follow-through, and consultancy in the workplace, a report on the results so far achieved was produced by those senior managers who had been directly involved. This report was one of the factors which led to a central management decision to extend the project throughout the Organisation.

In the report, many specific applications of Coverdale Training are cited, and it concludes with some observations on the pilot project by an outside observer: the Adviser on Training Projects of the Industry Training Board. He makes some points of general validity about the use and evaluation of Coverdale Training:

Coverdale Training, like other forms of Organisation Development, can only be assessed over a long time scale. Accordingly this document should be viewed as an interim report.

Reactions to the Coverdale Course (Part 1)
All managers interviewed were positive about the course. Reactions varied from warm to rapturous.
My observation was that the organisation felt more youthful and energetic. One manager confirmed this: 'There's a buzz of liveliness that I didn't sense a month ago.'
However, putting the learning to use in day-to-day business is less straightforward . . . . . .
The right kind of follow-up help by a Coverdale consultant and personal coaching by the senior manager are both essential for new skills and knowledge to be used.

Management Behaviour
Many changes in attitudes and behaviour have taken place. Often these are subtle, and sometimes not recognised by the manager concerned.
Managers have questioned their assumptions; about themselves, their colleagues and working practices. There have been several incidents when a long held belief was tested and found to be invalid.
The boundaries of what is perceived to be possible have been extended.
Managers are relating differently towards their bosses. One manager was emphatic about improved management teamwork in these words: 'Previously it was like going into the holy of holies, but what we did in the last meeting was entirely different!' More ideas are being generated, and there is a real sense of increased participation. At the end of a recent meeting one manager said: 'We've said it in the corridor outside, and I want to say it now—we feel more a part of it all now'. Extensive changes are taking place between managers on roughly the same status level. There is more time being taken to check understanding, identify common aims, and identify improvements in the skills of working together on business problems. One manager put it this way: 'You must be conscious of your objectives. This must be clear to everyone on the project. We did not do this before.' Managers are behaving differently to their subordinates and hourly paid staff. More time is taken in explanation, and individual targets are being set and measures of performance made known.

Management by Objectives
In a very real sense there is a movement towards a form of management by objectives approach in the units involved in the training project. However, this is growing organically from within the management teams, not imposed from the outside. Recently, objective-setting has been extended from a team approach to take in individual managers. The result of this shift of emphasis cannot yet be determined.

Discussion
The Coverdale Training Programme has stimulated many changes in working activity which are seen by managers to be constructive and liberating.
I agree with this view, and rate the effort as an unusually successful venture in management development.
Most benefit has been achieved when there has been active involvement of senior managers, careful follow-up of participants and feedback to the Company Personnel Office of the results of each aspect of the programme.[9]

I wish to express my gratitude to the late Ralph Coverdale for his help. He prepared an outline of the historical development of Coverdale Training, read several drafts of this chapter, and made many useful comments. I have taken account of them in the chapter as it stands.

My thanks too to all the consultants of The Coverdale Organisation. Their experience has been the basis of what is described here.

While the method and themes of Coverdale Training are common to all Coverdale consultants, this description of them is a personal one.

References

1. Seamus G. Roche and John Waterston, 'Coverdale Training: Building on Ability', p. 47, *Training and Development Journal*, February 1972, published by the American Society for Training and Development, Inc.
2. Page 9, 'Examples of Application Reported by Delegates to the First Three Preparatory (Part I) Courses in F.A.O.', 3 July 1972, distributed within F.A.O. by Coverdale Training Ltd.
3. Pages 2–3, 'Evaluation of the effectiveness of a Coverdale Training Course' by Neil Ferguson. Behavioural Sciences Research Division (C.S.D.) report No. 2, 1971.
4. Pages 1–2 (Summary), Ferguson, *op. cit*.
5. Page 1, 'Digest of a Report on a Coverdale Project in a Process Industry', by John Williams, Coverdale Training Limited, March 1972.
6. Page 3, *Ibid*.
7. Page 3, *Ibid*.
8. Page 4, Williams, *op. cit*.
9. Annexure III in 'Report on Trial of Coverdale Training', April 1972, published for internal use by a national production and distribution company.

© John Waterston

CHAPTER 3

The Study of the Small Group in an Organisational Setting

BY B. W. M. PALMER

My aim in this paper is to describe the study of behaviour in small groups, as it is practised within the courses and conferences developed by the Tavistock Institute of Human Relations, and subsequently by other institutions including my own. Strictly the word 'conference' refers in this paper to residential courses, and the word 'course' to non-residential courses. However, I have sometimes used one word to stand for both, to avoid repeating the cumbersome expression 'conferences and courses'. These have developed from the work of A. K. Rice and his colleagues at the Centre for Applied Social Research[a], one of the constituent centres within the Tavistock Institute of Human Relations. Most of the experience on which the paper is based was gained in conferences and courses sponsored by the Grubb Institute of Behavioural Studies, in collaboration with the Centre for Applied Social Research and independently. I have also taken part in conferences organised by the C.A.S.R. alone (the 'Leicester' conference), the Ministry of Transport (as it then was), and the University of Bristol.

I wish to thank P.M. Turquet of the Centre for Applied Social Research for reading the final draft of this paper, and for his detailed and helpful comments. I have taken account of these in the final revision. While this paper represents in broad terms the standpoint of the C.A.S.R. and my own Institute, the particular account is my own, and would not necessarily receive the assent of my colleagues in these institutions in every respect.

The Setting of the Small Group Event

A Small Group (or Study Group) consists of between eight and twelve people usually referred to as 'members', and one who is designated as 'consultant'. An associate consultant or observer is sometimes present as a trainee. The group meets for a variable number of $1\frac{1}{2}$ hour sessions—between six and about thirteen in the conference setting. The members are given basic information about dates and times of sessions, venue, and the names of the participants, and a written statement of the task of the group and of the consultant.

---

*Superordinate letters (a), (b), (c) refer to sections of the Postscripts.

The task of the group is to study its own behaviour as a group as it happens. The task of the consultant is to assist the group in its task.

The Small Group is not a leaderless group. Although he does not give the kind of lead which some expect of him, the consultant's contributions are consistently directed towards enabling the members of the group to examine and try to understand the group's behaviour.

In this paper I shall be concerned with Small Groups which constitute one of the events in the programme of a working conference on group behaviour. This may be a 1 or 2-week residential conference, or a 1-week non-residential conference forming part of a 6-month programme of intermittent events. Courses consisting entirely of Small Groups are also organised, with meetings once a week or on successive evenings.

The typical 2-week conference consists of about 70 members and 12 staff, the 1-week conference of 50 members and 9 staff. The titles have changed over the years, as the focus of study has shifted and been more precisely defined: 'Group Relations', 'Learning for Leadership', 'Leadership and Authority', 'Authority and Organisation'.

Members are recruited from a wide range of professions and spheres of work: industry and commerce, the medical and social services, government, education, the churches, and others. They are generally in positions of authority in their own work, and many receive financial support from their organisations in attending a conference. The staff are drawn from the sponsoring Institute and other organisations. The 6-month 'Behaviour in the Working Environment' courses have so far comprised 30–40 members and about 8 staff. A distinctive feature of these courses is the time given to the continuing study of members' own working problems. Each course is built up of groups of 4–10 members of the same profession, who work together on issues of common concern.

The first conference to be run in the United Kingdom was organised jointly by the Tavistock Institute of Human Relations and the University of Leicester in 1957. In this conference the small groups were the central event: 'The small face-to-face group was seen from the beginning as the main laboratory for the study of group relations'.[1] Later, under the directorship of Rice, the study of large group and inter-group behaviour was given equal prominence in the programme. Two forms of Inter-Group event were used, one for the study of relations between groups formed by members, the other also called the Institutional Event, for the study of relations between members and staff within the total conference institution. If any event can now be called the main event it is this last one, since the conferences are now seen to be concerned with behaviour within institutions or organisations.

The 1957 conference included application work, which provided opportunities to apply insights gained to working problems. Subsequent residential conferences have also included sessions for application work, but it is recognised that these can do no more than initiate the process of translating the experience of the conference into understanding which is applicable at work. The 'Behaviour in the Working Environment' course, which is still at the experimental stage, is an attempt to solve the problem of application. It includes regular consultations on working problems with staff consultants.

The Practitioners

The early Leicester conferences brought together the psychoanalytic approach to the understanding of groups developed by W. R. Bion and others at the Tavistock Clinic and Institute, and concepts of training in group relations developed at the National Training Laboratory in Group Development at Bethel, Maine, and its allied institutions. They were an expression of the aim of the Tavistock Institute, of relating a psychoanalytic understanding of the personality and behaviour of the individual to other disciplines concerned with the structural social group. When Rice took over the directorship of the Leicester conferences in 1962, they diverged increasingly from the methods and ethos of the N.T.L. The conferences continued to work with and develop Bion's theory of small group behaviour, but also incorporated the concepts of organisations developed through Rice's parallel work as a management consultant, with others at the Institute. Since his death the Leicester conferences have continued under the direction of E. J. Miller and P. M. Turquet.

Similar conferences and courses have been run by the Grubb Institute of Behavioural Studies since 1963. In that year Bruce Reed, the Director of the Grubb Institute, invited Rice to direct a jointly-sponsored conference. The first staff consisted of Rice, Turquet, Reed, R. W. Herrick of the Anglican Diocese of Chelmsford, and Miss Jean Hutton of the Grubb Institute. This group, with the later addition of myself, provided the nucleus of the staff of subsequent residential conferences.

A number of other individuals and institutions have organised programmes of courses and conferences run along these lines, including Denis Rice at Leicester, Elizabeth Richardson at the University of Bristol, R. W. Herrick in Chelmsford Diocese, and those associated with the A. K. Rice Institute in the United States.

Aims

In a recent brochure the aim of the course was stated in these terms:

Our aim is to help those with responsibility for management to understand better how people behave in their particular working environment, so that they can make more informed decisions, and perhaps act as informal advisers to their colleagues and institutions. We are not attempting to train specialists in the behavioural sciences. Our aim is that people like headmasters, prison governors, social workers, clergy and industrialists should be able to adapt the language and methods of the specialists for their own use, and thus enrich their own way of working.[2]

Our hope for those who participate in our courses and conferences is therefore that they should be more effective in planning, organising, directing, supporting and controlling the activities of their institutions or departments — more effective, in other words, in their role as managers.

More specifically, the conferences themselves are designed to facilitate a task defined as: 'to provide opportunities to learn about the nature of authority, and the inter-personal and inter-group problems encountered in exercising it'.[3] An earlier formulation by Rice refers to 'providing opportunities to learn about leadership'.[4] Emphasis upon the concept of leadership tends to focus attention upon the skills and qualities of leaders. Rice distinguished three elements in leadership which were developed through conferences:

> Leadership involves sensitivity to the feelings and attitudes of others, ability to understand what is happening in a group at the unconscious as well as the conscious level, and skill in acting in ways that contribute to, rather than hinder, task performance. But increased sensitivity and understanding are means, not ends, and the end is the production of more effective leaders and followers.[4]

More recent conferences have focused upon the nature of the authority which is vested in those who take leadership roles, as well as upon the skills which those who take leadership roles are required to exercise. Participants frequently explore the difference between leadership which is exercised with the authority of a group or institution, and that which is exercised through the personal power, influence or charisma of the individual.

The aim of the Small Group has a corresponding focus. In general terms it is to learn about the behaviour of small groups which form part of a larger institution; more specifically there is the opportunity to examine the relatively simple authority relationships which arise in this setting, and the feelings and fantasies which characterise them.

Theoretical Assumptions

The theoretical framework upon which the conferences are based, and within which the staff work in the Small Group and other events, incorporates elements from a number of sources:

(a) Kurt Lewin's field theory of human behaviour, particularly its account of the interrelations between group and environment;[5,6]
(b) the concept of the consultant's, or analyst's, interpretation, as an elucidation of processes taking place in the 'here and now', first put forward by Strachey[7] and an essential element in Bion's approach to the study of groups (see below);
(c) the Kleinian theory of the development of personality,[8,9] and other concepts employed by the object relations school of dynamic psychology;
(d) W. R. Bion's theory of behaviour in small groups;[10]
(e) the open system approach to the study of organisations.[11,12] This approach views organisations as systems of interdependent activities, which persist and develop through the exchange of human and material resources, energy, and information with their environment. (Some models of organisations are in effect closed system models: they imply that the organisation is independent of its environment.)

It is beyond the scope of this paper to discuss these theories in detail. In what follows I shall indicate the bearing of some key concepts upon the study of small groups in the conference setting.

Bion states that in any small group it is possible to discern two types of mental activity[b]. The nature of the mental activity, the kind of thinking which is going on, is inferred from what group members say and do. The first he called sophisticated or work-group activity, using W as an abbreviation for work-group. I shall use the expression 'W-activity'. This is rational co-operative activity directed towards carrying out the task which the group has been constituted to perform. The effectiveness of any working group depends upon the capacity of its members to engage in this kind of activity, in the face of whatever personal or circumstantial difficulties they have to contend with.

This activity, Bion writes:

... is obstructed, diverted, and on occasion assisted, by certain other mental activities that have in common the attribute of powerful emotional drives. These activities, at first sight chaotic, are given a certain cohesion if it is assumed that they spring from basic assumptions common to all the group.[13]

These 'basic assumption activities' are regarded by Bion as defences against the primitive anxieties which are aroused in the individual by the complexities of life in a group. They may be seen as means of defending the individual against feelings of impending chaos or obliteration, by securing the *survival* of the group.

Bion noted the concern of groups with their own survival at an early stage in his study of small groups:

... what is the basic assumption in a group about people who meet together in a group? The basic assumption is that people come together as a group for purposes of preserving the group.[14]

In my own Institute we have come to emphasise this survival element in group behaviour, and have begun to speak of 'S-activity' rather than basic assumption activity.

In a group dominated by S-activity, individuals show 'a capacity for instantaneous involuntary combination with one another',[15] and their behaviour suggests that they share the same unconscious images of, and assumptions about, the state of the group and its environment.

W-activity

W-activity is mental activity directed towards the attainment of objective, public ends by rational means. In a small working group it therefore includes defining the task (or tasks) which the group has been constituted to perform, identifying the resources needed to carry it out, defining the roles which have to be performed, and allocating members to those roles. It entails setting goals, monitoring progress, and assessing results.

In many approaches to the study of group behaviour, the groups are usually set up so that their meetings are as far as possible undisturbed by the outside world. There is therefore a tendency to regard them as closed systems. The performance of a task is then thought of as an internal activity. If this model of the experimental group is taken as a point of departure for thinking about all small working groups they then tend to be treated as though they were closed systems too.

It is more satisfactory to regard a group as a small organisation which persists as a social entity through regulated exchanges with its environment — that is, as an open system. This model is implicit in Bion's writings, since he regards the co-operative W-activity of the group as analogous to the activity of the ego in the individual personality; the ego is that function of the personality which regulates the individual's adaptation to his environment. Every group therefore has its 'imports' from its environment, and its 'exports' which it returns to the environment. This is readily seen in the case of a manufacturing department in a factory, which takes in raw materials from suppliers and converts them into exported products and waste. The model is also applicable to working groups whose imports and exports are people.

Within this frame of reference, leadership in W-activity may be defined as a function which facilitates task performance by regulating exchanges between the group (or organisation) and its external world. As such its exercise is not restricted to one designated leader: it is a function which each member performs according to his role in the group.

W-activity, and in particular the exercise of any leadership role, makes emotional demands upon the individual. The experience of these demands, and of the ways in which they are evaded, is an important element in this form of training. The performance of any task entails tolerance of the anxiety, concern, guilt or disappointment which accompanies making decisions on incomplete information and awaiting the outcome; or seeing plans which seemed good in conception only partially realised; or making changes; or making mistakes; or making choices which benefit some and harm others; or taking action which arouses antagonism in others; or terminating projects and organisations which have completed their task or been unable to do so. The list could be extended. Insofar as he is able to tolerate these feelings, the individual is able to sustain W-activity. Similarly a group needs to be able to tolerate these feelings amongst its members, in order to be able to go on working. However, it appears that beyond a certain threshold of tolerance an individual or a group instinctively takes steps to mitigate the anxieties which are being aroused. In face of what is felt to be impending catastrophe, there is a resort to various defensive manoeuvres, that is, to S-activity.

W-activity, on the part of individual or group, entails constructing a conceptual map, or working model, of the group and its environment (for the notion of conceptual maps and working models, see Bowlby[16] and Laing.[17] It may be built up mentally or set down in words, diagrams and other symbols. Effective task performance depends upon the match between working model and reality; if this is adequate the individual or group is able to predict the outcomes of alternative courses of action, and so make decisions which have the best possibility of success. This entails accepting that the working model cannot fully represent the actual state of affairs, and tolerating this uncertainty.

S-activity

The behaviour of people in groups frequently suggests that whatever sophisticated working model they share has been replaced or overlaid by a model or another order. Bion concluded that three basic models were able to account for the behaviour of the groups he studied:

(i) *Dependence*. The members of the group behave as if they are weak, vulnerable, ill-equipped children, depending for their survival upon some all-knowing, all-providing leader, institution or idea.

(ii) *Expectancy*. The members of the group behave as if they are also weak, vulnerable and ill-equipped, but live in hope of the advent of a new leader, institution or idea which will inaugurate a golden age in which the survival of the group will be assured. (Bion used the term 'pairing' for this model, because it frequently includes two individuals who are seen as the potential parents of the new leader. Rice regards (i) and (ii) as two variants of the same model.[18]

(iii) *Fight-flight*. The group behaves as if threatened by a malign and destructive person, institution or idea, which it must destroy or evade in order to survive.

In certain specialised groups these models are consciously affirmed as a reliable basis for W-activity; notably in religious meetings ((i) and (ii)) and in battles (iii). In ordinary working groups these models are generally unconscious and unacknowledged, but may be inferred from images which are used in discussion and from the pervading mood of the meeting.

When a group is dominated by S-activity, the behaviour of its members is powerfully directed towards maintaining the current model of its world. Its capacity to perceive the real situation, internally and externally, is correspondingly impaired. The group superimposes or projects its images onto its surroundings, endeavouring not to test their validity but to mould reality into their shape. If the facts do not fit, so much the worse for the facts. The group is no longer open to new information or ideas, and is operating as though it were a closed system. Such behaviour obstructs task performance, and in the long term may jeopardise the survival of the group. In the short term, however, it replaces intolerable anxieties by anxieties which are more tolerable because they can be dissipated in activity, such as rousing the all-powerful leader to action, preparing for the dawning of the new age, or engaging in fight or flight.

The relationship between S-activity and W-activity

While individuals in a group may oscillate between S-activity and W-activity, according to the adequacies of their skills, the feasibility of the task, the quality of the leadership, and many other factors, the group as a group seems to resist transitions between the two. When the members of a group have combined in S-activity the individual who introduces a spirit of enquiry or concern for facts poses a great threat and is subject to pressure to abandon his position. Similarly a group engaged in co-operative W-activity resists the individual who injects exaggerated hopes and fears into the proceedings. They are like climbers who are roped together and therefore able to support the member who slips. On the other hand, as in climbing, the one who slips sometimes pulls the rest of the group down with him.

It is sometimes supposed that these two kinds of activity correspond to the emotional and the intellectual or practical aspects of the group's behaviour. This is very misleading. W-activity derives its motive force from the feelings which run amok in S-activity. W-activity cannot be sustained without trust in leaders and representatives who are regarded as dependable. They are not, however, made in fantasy into infallible leaders and representatives; members are prepared to question how the authority which they have delegated is being exercised. Similarly W-activity demands hope and expectancy which do not prevent the facing of facts, and a capacity for controlled fight against, or withdrawal from, obstacles or opponents.

A group's fear of being overwhelmed by S-activity may be so great that it endeavours to reduce all expression of feeling and fantasy to a minimum. Definitions of task, role and procedure are used, not primarily as aids to task performance, but as bulwarks against invasion by 'undisciplined squads of emotion'. This defensive use of organisation results in the extreme case in simulated work which has the appearance of sophistication but which is more appropriately regarded as another expression of S-activity. This defence is familiar to us in conferences, in which an increasing number of members have some knowledge of how staff and members behave in such conferences, and simulate this stereotyped behaviour very skilfully, as a defence against the disruption of further learning.

It may be worth adding that the distinction between W- and S-activity in groups is not the same as the distinction which is sometimes drawn between content and process. Our terms both refer to the type of mental activity which is taking place. This manifests itself both in the verbal content of any discussion, and in the process of interaction which takes place between group members. To assess whether W- or S-activity predominates in a group it is necessary to take account of both content and process.

Assumptions about Learning

The conferences, and the Small Group event within them, embody assumptions, not only about group processes, but also about the process of learning. Indeed, for some people, attending a conference is probably as important for learning about learning, as for learning about groups.

The conferences are designed to provide opportunities for learning by experience. Earlier conferences included lectures, but these were discontinued in the residential conferences several years ago. This does not mean that we believe that it is only necessary to experience the problems of exercising authority in groups, to learn how to overcome them. If this were so it would not be necessary to run conferences. The assumption we make is that learning takes place through the 'marriage' of an experience and an idea which gives form to the experience. The idea (which may be a name, an image, or a more abstract concept) gives a shape to the experience; the experience gives content or meaning to the idea.[19,20] For instance, a group member has unpleasant feelings which are given coherence by the idea that he feels like a child who has been reprimanded by his headmaster. This image enables him to examine the situation further; who is the headmaster? In what ways is his situation like that of a child? Further contributions in the group might show that there is a pervasive sense of having become like children. This might provide immediate content to the conception of a group which sees its members as weak and ignorant, depending upon an all-knowing leader—an example of S-activity characterised by a shared assumption of dependence. At this stage members may begin to make cross-references to other situations in which this model has dominated people's thinking.

It is possible to expound the idea of S-activity dependence in a lecture, or in a paper as I have done briefly here. This may be understood as an idea by the hearer or reader, but it does not follow that it will come to mind when he is actually involved in the kind of relationships to which the term refers. The assumption we make is that the idea is more likely to come to mind if it is married to experience of the phenomena it refers to.

We are not interested in simply being able to label experiences. We further assume that experiences which can be named and located within larger systems of concepts can then be thought about. A manager may have been experiencing the problems of exercising authority in a group for many years, but learned very little about how to cope with them. Through a conference of this kind he learns a language for talking and thinking about his experience as a manager. This makes it possible for him to think out new approaches to recurring situations and to try them out. As an important by-product it also makes these situations less anxious for him: once they can be described they are reduced to manageable proportions.

We thus assume that there is the greatest potentiality for learning where concepts can be introduced close to the experiences to which they refer. Conferences and laboratories are not the only contexts in which this can take place. In consultancy work there are opportunities to help clients to interpret their on-going working experience; this is the basis of the Consultation Groups which are included in the 'Behaviour in the Working Environment' course. A lecturer may so know his listeners' world that he is able to evoke vivid memories of experiences, which he can then marry with the concepts he is putting forward. We thus view the conference as one of a number of possible contexts in which learning about group processes can take place.

The Method of the Small Group: an Illustration

Several accounts have been written of the kind of interaction which takes place in Small Groups[21,22] and Bion's descriptions of the therapeutic groups through which he developed his original theory are still highly illuminating. None of these accounts convey quite the atmosphere or the dominant preoccupations of Small Groups in which I have recently taken part, and I propose to supplement them with a brief account of my own. I shall describe two consecutive sessions of a Small Group in which I acted as consultant during a 'Behaviour in the Working Environment' course in 1972.

The group consisted of eight men and three women drawn from the prison service, probation hostels, education, churches, and business. We met in a pleasantly decorated room in a university hall of residence, sitting on moderately comfortable stacking chairs in a compact circle. The sessions I shall describe were the fourth and fifth of a series of seven, and took place from 9.30 to 11.00 a.m. and 11.30 a.m. to 1.00 p.m. on the third day of the conference, which was non-residential. The dominant theme of the first session, as I saw it, was that of members' feelings about coming back to the course and the group at the beginning of the day, and the ways in which they sought to create a group in which the conflicting demands upon their time and commitment which the course created could be somehow made of no account. The second session seemed to revolve around their hostility towards me, as one who represented at that moment the conflicting demands which anyone in a position of authority has to sustain.

I went in punctually at 9.30 a.m. to find only four members present. The others trickled in during the next 10 minutes, except for Mr. A. who had said the day before that he had another engagement and arrived about an hour later. The intial rather fragmentary discussion was concerned with who was late and why. This was a change from the session the previous morning, when lateness had been ignored and the intial discussion had been about the Inter-Group event. I commented on the fact that they were now using the word 'late', and shortly afterwards that as a result they had now to face the fact that it was difficult to work with several absentees. I was hoping to help them to see that, having formed an idea of a group which had time-limits—that is, a group with a boundary—they were now having to face whatever was inside that boundary.

Latecomers talked about what it was like coming late. Mr. B. had imagined himself being told to go away. (Mr. A., when he eventually arrived, said that although he had said he could be late, he hung about for several minutes outside, for fear of having to explain himself.) Miss C. said she had been glad she was with another member of the course, presumably since this gave her an alibi. It was pointed out to her that she had avoided taking the chair next to me, choosing to sit between the other two women. She said she had sat where the ash-tray was, then added: 'No, that's not true, I didn't want to sit next to the consultant.' Several people supplied an explanation: 'You wanted to be able to see him, see what he is doing.' I felt that I had become a dangerous object to the group, perhaps someone who would take them to task for being late, and made this comment. If I had been clearer I might have added that the idea of lateness had originated with group members, but that they were now making me into the dangerous, reprimanding person so that they could build up the idea of a welcoming group which it was good to come back to.

Mr. D., a clergyman, said he would have to be 5 minutes late every day because of a service he was committed to take every morning. (He was in fact on time the next day.) Another clergyman, Mr. E., said that he had given notice when he joined the course that he would be away on Thursday. Mr. B. said that he could have hurried to the course, but had stayed chatting to his wife. I felt, and commented, that there was a wish to establish that lateness and absence were due to immutable external factors or compelling loyalties. This covered up the fact that people made choices about priorities, accepting the demands of one person or group and rejecting those of another. In my mind was the notion that W-activity requires choices of this kind, and tolerance of the accompanying feelings of guilt and uncertainty. Because the members could not tolerate these feelings, they were engaging in collusive S-activity to suppress them. I suggested that there had been no reference to Mr. A., who had not yet arrived, or their feelings about him, because this might bring into the open their own uncertainties about attendance.

When Mr. A. eventually arrived he was greeted and then ignored for a while. When he was later questioned, he delivered a long tirade, about the situation he had been dealing with in connection with his work, and then about the 'little girl in the office', that is, the conference office, whom he had told he would be away. She had heard what he had to say, but had not given him any reassurance that he was doing the right thing (this is how the conference secretary would normally respond to such communications). The group pilloried Mr. A. for this, telling him at some length that it was up to him to take responsibility for his own actions. Their severity towards him probably stemmed from an awareness that he was undercutting the position they had been building up, which was that people had external commitments and needed to have no qualms about giving them priority. They were also giving him exactly the kind of ticking off which other latecomers had said they had feared, and were thus acting out the fantasy of a reprimanding authority which had pervaded the session.

Sitting in his customary position 6 inches back from the circle, Mr. D. then stated that he made up his own mind about his priorities and accepted personal responsibility for the decisions he made. In the comment I made I took some care to distinguish between the general validity of this statement, which I did not question, and its significance in the context of this meeting now. Here it seemed to be another expression of the search of a group for a formula which would solve their problems about conflicting priorities, and hence a manifestation of S-activity. In this case, as the withdrawn chair symbolised, the formula was to avoid an entangling involvement with the group which might mean painful choices of priority.

Mr. F. started to express dissent from what I had said. While he was speaking I noticed by my watch that it was past eleven o'clock. I had overrun the end of the session by a minute or more. I stood abruptly and left while Mr. F. was still speaking. It is usual for the consultant to observe starting and finishing times precisely in Small Groups, but I would not normally walk out while someone was speaking. My behaviour therefore suggests that I had also picked up the idea of a severe, clock-watching authority who would take me to task for my lateness.

I entered the second session on time, and without deliberate thought sat next to Mr. F., the man on whom I had walked out. Several members were up to a minute late. Mrs. G. talked about the need for flexibility in one's work, and the theme was taken up by Mr. E. and others. I said I thought the group were angry with me for walking out while Mr. F. was talking, and that I had in fact overrun time and was wondering why I had become so absorbed in the discussion. Members confirmed that they were angry; my further comment was not taken up for some time. Mr. A. referred to the need in any situation for good relationships to be established with whoever constituted the management. I said I thought good relationships here meant that I should join the group and adapt to its timing (S-activity), rather than to stick to my task of helping to study whatever happened between the scheduled times of 9.30 and 11 o'clock (W-activity). The distinction in my mind was between a working organisation which met between the times stated in the programme, in which I was a participant, and a social group or 'sentient group' which had formed within this structure, which members wished to preserve, which I would not join when its activities conflicted with those of the working organisation.

Mr. H. said that my leaving on time gave them an opportunity for discussion among themselves, but this was not taken up. The meeting was at that time conforming to the idea of an outraged group confronting a hostile and inflexible representative of management.

My leaving was compared by Miss J. with a plenary meeting of members and staff earlier in the course, which the staff had left early. Although reasons for this had been given, subsequent events in the course showed that this had been felt to be an expression of extreme disapproval on the part of the staff, which could not be forgotten. Although I did not recognise it at the time, we were now seeing in the Small Group how one episode in the life of an institution affects how another is perceived. My walking out on Mr. F. conjured up a fantasy which was saturated with feelings of condemnation, hostility and lack of care. By unconsciously carrying this fantasy over into the present situation, the group gave themselves an object, the consultant, on whom they could discharge their anger (S-activity). In order to respond rationally to the present situation (W-activity), the group would have had to explore what exactly had happened at the end of the previous session, and what therefore they had grounds for being angry about.

Miss J. said that some members might have wished that some staff members had stayed behind when the others left the plenary meeting. I suggested that there might also be a wish here to split me from my colleagues in the staff and get me to join these members. Mrs. G. said that I was in a bind: I was like a head-teacher who is answerable to County Hall as well as to her own school. Miss J. linked me with a Tavistock Institute consultant who had stressed the importance of sticking to rules about time in her hostel. I said I thought that they were now picturing me as a slave of some external authority such as the management of the course, or the theories of the Tavistock Institute, so that they would not have to see me as *choosing* to leave, or personally endorsing the theory behind leaving. They wanted an impersonal extension of the management, not Barry Palmer. Mr. D. asked whether one could be hostile to a role without being hostile to the person? He seemed to think one could; I was trying to show that they wanted to ignore what they felt to be true (S-activity), which was that Barry Palmer was hostile to them as persons, and they were hostile to him.

At this point I think in retrospect that my comments began to show signs of S-activity too. To make clear that I believed their hostility to be directed towards me as a person, I suggested that at that moment it might well be focused upon my tone of voice, my appearance, or my mannerisms (I remembered that my own hostilities tend to find a focus in irritations of this kind). I believe now that, by making these comments I was actively creating a group hostile to myself, rather than simply examining the meaning of hostility which was already present. This distinction is not a wholly clear one; nevertheless I would say that I was at this point beginning to collude with the emergence of fight-flight S-activity, and therefore losing my capacity to contribute to W-activity within the group.

However, I regard the episode I have described as a potentially valuable one. Mrs. G.'s comparison of my position with her own as a headmistress suggests that other members too might have been putting themselves in my shoes, comparing my relationship to the conference staff and to the group with similar patterns of relationship in which they were involved. They showed the difficulty they had in tolerating the conflicting loyalties inherent in their roles, by trying to see me as a victim of the situation, with no responsibility in the matter.

I do not wish to continue this account of the session, which moved into another phase at about this point. The end of the session was, however, interesting. I was anxious not to walk out while someone was speaking. At a few moments before one o'clock Mr. K. started to speak. I waited a minute or more for him to finish and, as I left, pointed out that when I did wait, the group produced the longest contribution in its history. I think they and I were relieved to be able to laugh.

The Method of the Small Group: General Conception

1. THE ENVIRONMENT OF THE SMALL GROUP

The Small Group takes place in the context of a larger training institution, that of the total course or conference. As the above example shows, feelings and fantasies about incidents outside the Small Group are imported into it, and influence internal relationships. The Small Group provides an opportunity to examine how this happens. Insofar as they accept and value the task of the Small Group, consultant and members exercise control over the way external factors are evoked in the group. In the above example, I used what had been said about the plenary meeting to explain the feelings which were now being expressed about my walking out on Mr. F. I am not sure whether Miss J. was also attempting to explain the group's present feelings, or whether she was directing attention to what had happened in the plenary meeting to obliterate the boundary between the Small Group and other events.

It is possible for members to feel so uncertain about the reliability of the basic arrangement for the course, that they are too preoccupied with these to be able to commit themselves to the work of the Small Group at all. We are therefore as thoughtful and reliable as we can be about the administrative arrangements, seeing, for example, that members have up-to-date lists of who is taking part, a clear time-table, and all necessary information about meals, car parking, telephones and so on. Unexpected as the behaviour of the staff frequently is, members can be sure which staff members will be where at what times, and what tasks they will be endeavouring to pursue. Through providing an environment for the working sessions which is, while not perfect, a 'good enough' environment (to use Winnicott's term[23]), we enable members to tolerate and learn from the stresses which are generated within the working sessions.

2. THE ORGANISATION OF THE SMALL GROUP

The Small Group is not structureless or leaderless, although some members are initially more aware of forms of structure and leadership which are absent, than of those which are present. The time-table, venue, membership and task of each group is defined by the staff of the course and endorsed by the behaviour of the consultant. These definitions do not of course determine members' behaviour. How far they are endorsed or repudiated shows how far the authority of the staff is being endorsed or repudiated. Members' behaviour with respect to these definitions is an important focus of study, since it throws light upon the way boundaries and tasks are accepted or called into question in other organisations. As we have seen, there is a part of most conference members which would feel safer if the staff reprimanded those who were, according to the published time-table, late, and gave bouquets to those who tackled the published task in an approved fashion. Because this is not done they are seen to advocate a 'permissive' style of leadership. On the other hand, because the staff stick to times and tasks themselves, they are also seen as inflexible and authoritarian.

The staff sometimes collude with this move to make them into advocates or missionaries of a particular 'style' of leadership which, it is implied, is to be adopted and reproduced in other organisations whatever their task and circumstances. To the extent that they do this, they lose the opportunity to assist members in learning about the effects of different styles of leadership, by examining when a particular style assists the work of a group and when it does not.

3. THE ROLE OF THE CONSULTANT

The role of the consultant, like the role of mother, priest, manager, or psychoanalyst, is learned by seeing other people do it, primarily from the receiving end, and then by doing it oneself, sometimes with an initial period of supervision. It is therefore learned as a totality, and any analysis of what the consultant does is necessarily secondary and incomplete. It is true of the consultant role and of the courses as a whole, that we are continually endeavouring to discover and understand what we are already doing.

The task of the consultant in a Small Group is to help the members of the group to study the behaviour of the group. When in doubt what to do or say this is ultimately his only criterion for deciding, although he may take refuge in doing what has been done before or what receives the group's approval. He pursues this task in a number of ways. First, he endeavours continuously to put into words his own immediate awareness of what is currently happening, why it is happening, and what evidence there is to support his view. His most important evidence is what is happening to himself, as I have attempted to show in my example. Many of his comments are less comprehensive than this, as my example also demonstrates, but I believe the consultant may fail to help the members to see coherence and meaning in what is going on, unless he is all the time working towards a construction of this kind, and is recognised to be doing so.

Bion, since his observations about the behaviour of groups were published, has examined the nature and function of interpretations in psychoanalysis.[24] His conclusions have bearing upon the consultant's contributions in a Small Group. He suggests that interpretations have many different functions and attempts to classify them. They include giving a name to a previously unnamed phenomenon, taking note of a phenomenon which may prove to be significant; floating a possible construction on what is happening, to see whether it evokes confirmatory or contradictory responses; and putting forward a construction which is believed to be true, as a means of bringing about change in the pattern of relationships and the behaviour of the group.

He also points out that the ideas put forward in an interpretation, or indeed in any statement, may be primitive and concrete or in varying degrees more sophisticated and abstract. The latter evolve out of the former. In this section of this paper I started with a story about a particular Small Group, in which some of the underlying concepts were implied but not explicit, and have now moved to some more generalised statements which may have more meaning because of the more concrete ideas which came first. My aim in the Small Group, which is very imperfectly realised, is to pick up and elaborate images conceived by individuals, which express how the group see their shared situation and what they feel about it; and from these to develop more precise concepts which can be later used to describe other groups besides the present one.

The consultant is not simply a commentator, since he is an active participant in the group process. He exercises leadership, in the sense that by his words and behaviour he defines a task, adheres to it, and demonstrates how to go about it. A commentator has no responsibility for what happens whereas the consultant is accountable to the Director of the conference for making the best use of the opportunities for learning provided by the meetings of the group to which he is consultant. He recognises that his own behaviour influences the direction which the group takes, and endeavours to behave in a way which enables members to discover and face facts, rather than one which reinforces their fear of what the facts may be. As he does this he evokes in the group feelings and fantasies about himself as an authority figure, which it is an essential part of his task to help them to articulate and examine.

4. THE ROLE OF THE MEMBERS

Those who are accepted for a course and pay their fee have the status of members of the course. However, it comes as a surprise to most to discover that there is a role appropriate to members within each event, which they do not automatically recognise and adopt simply by attending the sessions. In virtually every Small Group, members complain that they do not know what the task is, or that there is no task, even when they are able to quote the definition of the task which is given in the brochure. What they are saying, I believe, is that they do not know what their role is, and therefore they cannot engage with the task. They do not know what to look for, what kind of contribution to make; they cannot imagine what understanding the behaviour of the group would be like. The behaviour of the consultant is equally baffling. It is only as they begin to experience gaining insight into the behaviour of the group that the nature of the overall task, the role of the consultant, and the role of members, begin to have some content for them.

The role of a student in a lecture is largely a receptive one, but the role of a member of a Small Group involves contributing, selectively, information about his current feelings, fantasies and perceptions. This information is raw material from which consultant and members are able to construct a view of the state of the group as a total system. The member role involves evaluating the perceptions and interpretations of other members and of the consultant in the light of his own experience. It involves putting forward his own view of the group's behaviour to test his own understanding. In practice this role is often difficult to maintain. The member is swamped by his own and others' fears of being seen to be incompetent or ignorant, resentment at being dependent upon other people to learn, and alarm at what comes to light. This experience is itself valuable raw material for learning about the problems of subordinates, pupils, followers and clients.

Evaluation

In assessing the results of this kind of activity I shall not attempt to consider Small Groups apart from the courses and conferences of which they form a part.

In the related T-group field there have been a number of studies of their effect upon participants,[25] but I doubt very much whether those who conduct T-groups, or attend them, do so because of findings of this kind. Rice and Turquet planned a programme of research into the effects of the residential conferences.[26] It was to employ intensive interviewing of samples of individuals, on receiving the initial information about the conference, during the time between registering as members and entering the conference, and during a period following the conference. Applications for funds to carry out this study were unsuccessful, but as far as I know there was never any question of halting the conference programme until the research could be carried out.

Ultimately, however, the conferences must be judged according to the theoretical and applied studies to which they give rise. There is a growing body of literature, including both theoretical statements and applications to various spheres of work, in which the leading concepts were either born, or went through significant developments, in the courses I have described. A number of studies have been concerned primarily with industrial and commercial organisations;[12,27] others have examined problems of task, organisation and professional practice in education,[28,29,30,31,32] social work training,[33] residential work,[34] and churches.[35] Other writers have continued to develop concepts of the individual in relationship to the group.[36,37] The reader is referred to the books and papers listed[c].

The assessment made by participants

The immediate test of the usefulness of the courses remains the personal assessment of those who take part. For those of us who take part as staff, therefore, the test is whether we judge that we have learned from the courses, and continue to do so. We do not simply organise an institution in which we teach and the members learn. The conference is a learning milieu, in which new members, those who attend for a second time (sometimes working as a separate sub-conference), trainee staff, experienced staff, and those who act as director of the conference (or chairman of the staff group), have the opportunity to extend their own understanding of group processes, and of authority and leadership.

What is the nature of the learning which participants discern in themselves and in others? During courses one may observe marked changes in the behaviour of participants and in the insight they display. These signs of change provide encouragement to staff, and probably to members, in the heat of the day, but they are of minor significance. Changes of behaviour induced by the immediate experience of the course, and the feelings of satisfaction and dissatisfaction which accompany them, are usually ephemeral and misleading.

Of greater significance are the indications received subsequently, by staff, from participants and their colleagues at work, that lasting changes have taken place in their relationships with others or in their competence as leaders and followers. Success stories could be collected; their cumulative significance would be difficult to assess. There is a need, however, for some form of descriptive study, perhaps along the lines proposed by Rice and Turquet. It should focus upon members' working situation, and their behaviour in that situation before and after the course, rather than simply upon changes in their perceptions of themselves and others. My preference would be to build such a study into a course which included on-going consultative discussions, rather than basing it on a residential conference.

In the absence of such a study, the members' comments which conclude this paper will provide an indication of the terms in which members describe their own learning.

The changes which take place are sometimes experienced and described in personal terms. Participants find themselves to be generally less anxious, less inhibited, or more able to use their aggression overtly and constructively. These changes are gratifying, but a bonus as far as the organisers are concerned. If we were interested primarily in personal development, the conferences would not be designed in the way they are.

Our aim is to improve role-performance; that is, to make it possible for the individual to develop his capacity to engage in W-activity in the working groups of which he is a member. Our experience is that many participants gain awareness, not only of themselves, but of the processes, conscious and unconscious, which take place in groups and larger human systems. Those who take part in further conferences, theoretical discussions and consultation work are able to give this awareness greater conceptual sharpness. Participants are thus in different degrees better equipped to understand the situations that confront them, as managers and in other roles, day by day. They are consequently less likely to fall back upon S-activity as a means of dealing with uncertainty and stress, and in a better position to arrive at rational decisions and courses of action.

Effects of this kind are not always observable in the short term. Past course members have occasionally told us that it was only in a particularly demanding situation, like a major reorganisation of their establishment, that they became aware of the value of the course experience to them. Such long-term effects would be very difficult to trace back unambiguously to a course, in any research study.

It is not the usual practice of the Grubb Institute or the Centre for Applied Social Research to follow up members and ask them to evaluate the course in which they took part. We wish members to feel that they are free to make use of their experience in any way they choose, with no obligation to have any further relationship with us. We are also aware that member satisfaction is not necessarily an index of learning, so that the information provided by a follow-up study is of doubtful value. In spite of these doubts, the Grubb Institute has carried out one simple survey of course members' reactions.

Questionnaires were sent to those who had taken part in three 'Behaviour in the Working Environment' courses during the period 1969-71. The form provided included space for comment on various aspects of the course, such as programme, experiential events, Consultations Groups, and practical arrangements. I shall not discuss these comments.

Participants were also invited to comment on the effect of the course upon them. The following features of the replies are of interest:

1. The changes reported are predominantly in the realm of insight and attitude. The member sees his working situation in a new way. These are clear examples:

I believe that I examine my personal relationships more scrupulously and interpret my own role far more in relation to the whole institution and the groups of people within it, i.e. staff, scholars (Headmistress).

Clarification of what I am doing here, what roles the village gives me; what 'folk religion' is; why P.C.C. and village are not synonymous: what expectations each have about parish, about me as Rector (Anglican priest).

I am much more aware of myself in group situations and the role I am taking at any one time, e.g. the authoritarian leadership one, the enabling one, etc. I am much more aware of the total institution of the hospital—the various parts of the whole—their inter-relations together and as separate units, etc. My role is a much more powerful one within the institution than I realise (Head Medical Social Worker).

2. A smaller number specify action which they have taken as a result of the course. Some members obviously had more scope for making organisational changes than others:

I was convinced at the end of the course that the value of communication is in small groups, and have reduced the number of large meetings held in my region. The involvement of all members of the group has also become much more of a condition of mine (Assistant Principal Probation Officer).

Structural reorganisation of upper echelon of (County) Service looked at in Consultation Group most effectively. Suggestions about isolation of new appointment, decision making processes, etc., made as a direct result of the insights developed (Assistant Principal Probation Officer).

3. Several members comment on finding themselves more assertive, more aggressive, and sometimes less popular as a result:

Considerable effect . . . some of my clients may not see this as beneficial, may take the view that I am not being too 'helpful' on occasions! (Industrial training manager.)

I feel more mature, less conforming and I think not quite as nice! (Senior Child Care Officer.)

4. There were two or three comments which suggested that the course had had a negative effect, of which the clearest was that of a member who said that the course had had 'a considerable effect on his personal life':

My latent depressive side rose to the fore after the course and I blamed myself for all local church failure. Some blame was justified. The depressive illness in retrospect seems worthwhile (Free Church Minister).

5. One member had left his job:

Course helped me clarify my thinking in areas such as adequate staffing, clear job definition, etc., and the more I pressed for these the more the tensions rose, so that in the end I came to believe that the only course left was resignation (Warden of training centre).

Although an organisation which nominates a member may not be very satisfied if he resigns his post as a result, we do not necessarily regard this as an unsatisfactory outcome. A proportion of course members appear to be in the wrong job or the wrong organisation, and it is better for the individual and the organisation that this is recognised and appropriate action taken.

References

1. Trist, E. L. and Sofer, C., *Exploration in Group Relations*, Leicester University Press, 1959, p. 14.
2. *Behaviour in the Working Environment*, Introduction to the courses, Grubb Institute of Behavioural Studies, 1972, p. 3.
3. *Authority and Organisation*, Brochure for conference organised by the Grubb Institute of Behavioural Studies, January 1972, pp. 2 f.
4. Rice, A. K., *Learning for Leadership—Interpersonal and Intergroup Relations*, Tavistock, 1965, p. 5.
5. Lewin, K., *A Dynamic Theory of Personality*, McGraw-Hill, 1935.
6. Lewin, K., *Field Theory in Social Science*, Harper and Row, 1951.
7. Strachey, J., 'The Nature of the Therapeutic Action of Psychoanalysis', *Int. J. Psycho-Anal.* Vol. 15, 1934, pp. 127–59. Reprinted *Int. J. Psycho-Anal.* Vol. 50, 1969, pp. 275–92.
8. Klein, M., 'Our Adult World and its Roots in Infancy', in *Our Adult World and other Essays*, Heinemann, 1963.
9. Crowcroft, A., *The Psychotic*, Penguin, 1967, Chapter 4.
10. Bion, W. R., *Experiences in Groups*, Tavistock, 1961.
11. Emery, F. E. (Ed.), *Systems Thinking*, Penguin, 1969.
12. Miller, E. J. and Rice, A. K., *Systems of Organisation*, Tavistock, 1967.
13. Bion, W. R., ibid., p. 146.
14. Bion, W. R., ibid., p. 63.
15. Bion, W. R., ibid., p. 153.
16. Bowlby, J., *Attachment*, Hogarth Press and Institute of Psycho-Analysis, 1969, pp. 80 ff.
17. Laing, R. D., *The Politics of the Family*, Tavistock, 1971, pp. 3 ff.
18. Rice, A. K., ibid., p. 14 footnote.
19. Bion, W. R., *Learning from Experience*, Heinemann, 1962, especially Chapter 7.
20. Palmer, B. W. M., 'Thinking about Thought', *Human Relations* Vol. 26, no. 1, 1973, pp. 127–141.
21. Sutherland, J. D., 'The Study Group Method of Training', in Trist, E. L. and Sofer, C., ibid., p. 56.
22. Rice, A. K., ibid., Chapter 5.
23. Winnicott, D. W., *The Maturational Process and the Facilitating Environment*, Hogarth Press and Institute of Psycho-Analysis, 1966.
24. Bion, W. R., *Elements of Psycho-Analysis*, Heinemann, 1963, especially Chapters 5 and 6.
25. See review of research studies in Smith, P. B., *Improving Skills in Working with People: the T-group*, H.M.S.O., 1969, pp. 7 ff.
26. Rice, A. K., ibid., pp. 187 ff.
27. Rice, A. K., *The Enterprise and its Environment*, Tavistock, 1963.
28. Richardson, E., *The Environment of Learning*, Nelson, 1967, reprinted Heinemann, 1973.

29. Richardson, E., *Group Study for Teachers*, Routledge and Kegan Paul, 1967.
30. Rice, A. K., *The Modern University—A Model Organisation*, Tavistock, 1970.
31. Bazalgette, J. L., *Freedom, Authority and the Young Adult*, Pitmans Publishing, 1971.
32. Richardson, E., *The Teacher, the School and the Task of Management*, Heinemann, 1973.
33. Gosling, R., Miller, D. H., Turquet, P. M., and Woodhouse, D. L., *The Use of Small Groups in Training*, Codicote Press, 1967.
34. Miller, E. J. and Gwynne, G. V., *A Life Apart—a pilot study of residential institutions for the physically handicapped and the young chronic sick*, Tavistock, 1972.
35. Reed, B. D. and Palmer, B. W. M., 'The Local Church and its Environment', Contribution to Miller, E. J. (Ed.), *Task and Organisation*, memorial volume to A. K. Rice, John Wiley, 1976.
36. Turquet, P. M., 'Threats to Identity in the Large Group'. In Kreeger, L., (Ed.) *The Large Group: Therapy and Dynamics*, Constable, 1975.
37. Rice, A. K., *Individual Group and Inter-group Processes, Human Relations*, Vol. 22, No. 6, December 1969, p. 565

© 1979 B. W. M. Palmer

CHAPTER 4

Small Group Work in a Psychiatric Prison

BY B. MARCUS

Introduction

The psychiatric prison at Grendon Underwood was opened in 1962. It is part of the Prison Department's medical services and, going back a good way in time, the thinking that eventually led to its formulation was medical thinking;[1] more precisely a fusion of medical thinking with a humanitarian approach to penal problems, resulting in a belief that it was more profitable and more humane to think of certain deviant behaviours as calling for curative rather than punitive measures.

Accepting that, historically, medical and humanitarian influences were present at the birth of Grendon, it may be helpful to look at the present picture. Happily, the humanitarian underpinning is still there, and will be assumed throughout this chapter. But it will be interesting to look at the present picture to see how the medical assumptions have been modified. Certainly it is currently true that nearly 80 per cent of the intake (the present population is some 250 inmates), arrived because doctors in various parts of the prison system have said they should come to Grendon. It is possible, of course, that the inmates first brought themselves to a doctor's attention, but in the majority of cases the decision that sends people to Grendon is a medical decision. And indeed, the new arrival at Grendon could well imagine himself to be coming into a hospital type set-up. The Governor is called a Medical Superintendent, the core staff is mainly medical, and the medical ancillary staff is large. In theory, the medical model could have been adhered to in the treatment situation. The characteristic treatment activity could have been the familiar doctor–patient situation with the usual associated transactions — confidential sessions, prescription of drugs, etc., etc., with the remainder of the institutional population, that is the custodial staff, fulfilling disciplinary and medical ancillary roles. The reality is somewhat different. The characteristic treatment situation is not a two-person transaction with one person holding important specialist qualifications. It is rather a small group situation presided over by a prison officer innocent of any medical or psychological qualifications. Lay operated small group work is, in fact, the characteristic unit of treatment. Despite the medical-type history of Grendon's culture, the (predominantly medical) management has moved away from a sickness-like conception of criminal behaviour, and from a medical model for its correction; rather does it look like a social psychological model, with pressures exerted on individuals via small and large groups. New arrivals pick up more or less quickly that they are to look to groups of fellow-inmates as their primary helping agency, and indeed there is a strong tendency for the inmate culture to condemn individuals who try to establish a patient role for themselves by seeking medical-type attention—e.g. trying to see the doctors, asking for tranquilisers, sedatives, etc. The psychological health of a therapeutic unit tends to be negatively gauged by such criteria as the frequency of sick reporting, and the incidence of drug prescription,* and positively gauged by the readiness with which individuals talk to their groups, and with which the groups communicate to the larger community units.

Group work at Grendon, therefore, is not an excrescence; it goes on because in some way it fits in with a set of institutional assumptions. A good deal more will be said of this below, but in the meantime it would perhaps be better to put the horse before the cart. Group work is part of the institution's *conversion*† process, but it might have been more logical to start with the *import* material, i.e. the inmates.

The inmates are convicted criminals who somebody, usually a doctor, has considered, by uncertain criteria, to be suitable for referral. They are a highly recidivist population with an average—which has remained remarkably constant throughout Grendon's history—of eight previous convictions. Socially, they are a very downwardly mobile population, with a high incidence of people holding an occupational status lower than that of their fathers. Other signs of social inadequacy are not lacking—bad work records, marital breakdowns, alcoholism, etc. In short, they exhibit a good deal of socially deviant behaviour, including persistent criminality, but they do not exhibit breakdowns of psychotic dimensions—other institutions are considered more appropriate for such cases. Psychometric testing also shows them to be highly disturbed individuals, recording scores far higher than those said to be statistically normal on various tests of psychological maladjustment. It seems reasonable to assume that Grendon is dealing with a population far different from the ordinary run of citizens, but are they markedly different from the population where they are drawn—the general prison population? This is not certain. A comparison with a group of long-term prisoners (i.e. over 12 months) at Oxford Prison shows a marked similarity in severity of criminal history, indicating that, at any rate in this respect, Grendon men are no different from the general population of recidivist prisoners. But on

---

* Apparently justifiably so. In a recent follow-up study it was found that the highest reconviction rate occurred on a wing with the highest incidence of drug prescription.

† This author is here accepting Rice's[2] assumption that the organisation of any institution can be accommodated to the import–conversion–export model. In this instance the process by which disturbed criminals enter the system, go through the events that constitute 'treatment', and resume for 'normal' society.

psychometric testing, although there are some similarities, they appear to be more neurotic in an intro-punitive direction, and perhaps it is this that has tended to get them shunted into the direction of Grendon. If such testing is to be taken at its face value, it would appear that Grendon men, whilst as criminal as any bunch of men taken at random from a more conventional prison, may have a little more motivation to change their ways—although other data suggests that they have little in the way of psychological resources to implement their motivation.

The Treatment Philosophy

To provide something by way of external aid to assist this presumed genuine motivation, the institution's treatment ideology is offered. It is not difficult to see that what is practised at Grendon is something that pays strong allegiance to the treatment philosophy which it has been fashionable to call the therapeutic community. This aims to set up an institutional culture quite different from the conventional custodial culture. It is said by Maxwell Jones[3] to be distinguished by the unique way in which the total resources of the institution, staff and inmates, are mobilized in the interests of treatment. Maxwell Jones sets out what this means in terms of running the institution:

(a) *Active rehabilitation as against custodialism and segregation*—i.e. inmates participate in each other's treatment, they are not passive in relation to, and socially distant from, the staff.

(b) *Democratization as against hierarchies and status differentiation*—i.e. discussion and shared decision-making takes the place of 'doctor knows best' attitude; a diminution of difference towards rank or professional status.

(c) *Permissiveness, as against customary limitations on what may be said and done*—i.e. a loosening of traditional disciplinary structure, an atmosphere in which it is understood to be safe to say what one feels in the presence of people whose role is traditionally associated with control and punishment.

(d) *Communalism, as opposed to an emphasis upon the specialised role of the doctor*—i.e. treatment takes place in multiperson situations, small or large groups, not in the traditional doctor-patient dyadic situation. Therefore the doctor has to 'share' the therapeutic task with both the inmates, and other, non-professional, grades of staff.

Important ideas are implicit in these attitudes, and it will be useful to see how the operation of the small groups helps to promote these ideas. For example, the point has already been made that the most common treatment transaction is the prison-officer led small group. This is saying that a therapeutic task is undertaken by the sort of people whose role is conventionally expected to be custodial; this seems to be a contribution to what

Maxwell Jones calls 'communalism', it shares out the task of therapy instead of making it a specialisation prerogative of a small group of people with 'official' qualifications. It is also an important contribution to the therapeutic community ideal of the total resources of the unit being mobilised in the interests of treatment. Furthermore, important ideas about relationships to authority are implied in Maxwell Jones's list of attitudes—permissiveness, the greater permeability of hierarchical barriers, the lessening of social distances.

In considering here the possible helpfulness of small group work it will be convenient to think of the prison officer, in common with all front line staff in hierarchical systems, as being in the middle of a three-tier system; below him are the inmates, above him the institutional management—doctors, psychologists, etc. It is clear that the officer conducting a small group has of necessity to enter into a relationship with inmates very different from his customary disciplinary relationships. At a verbal level, at any rate, a freedom is attained which would be unthinkable in the habitual custodian-inmate relationship. A culture is created in which there are no longer things which must not be said (under penalty either of punishment from authority or ostracism by one's fellows). Here, obviously, a big step has been taken in the direction of permissiveness. (Since the *ultimate* aim of creating a certain kind of social climate is the behavioural betterment of the individual, it is worth making the point that an implied basic assumption of the whole set-up is the idea of transferability. This would mean that if officers and inmates operate within a framework of permissiveness, and the inmate becomes more kindly disposed towards authority figures within the institutional setting, this kindlier attitude is transferred to authority figures—e.g. employers—outside the prison setting. The likelihood of further anti-social behaviour would thereby be reduced. This may well be the weakest of all the Grendon assumptions—more of this below.) As regards the lessening of social distances upwards, the point is made now, and will be elaborated later, that a certain kind of management structure involving such lessened distances is needed if the officer is to see any point in his small group work (incidentally, no claim is necessarily made that libertarian ways of dealing with prison inmates have greater rehabilitative value than authoritarian ways, only that they provide a better social atmosphere for the functioning of small group work). Lastly, but perhaps most fundamentally, Maxwell Jones's definition of the therapeutic culture emphasises that the patients become active participants in their own therapy. Typically, people who talk about institutions (Barton,[4] Goffman[5]) assume that inmates of institutions passively have things done to and/or for them (Goffman, indeed, seems to say that not even therapeutic communities are an exception to this rule). In the therapeutic community, on the other hand, the patients are also the therapists, both for themselves and fellow-patients. It is hardly necessary to labour the point that, in the small group of therapeutic intent, given favourable conditions of operating, such patient-orientated therapeutic work does in fact happen—almost by definition, in fact since a favourably operating group would tend to be defined as a group in which the inmates were behaving therapeutically to each other. Patients in a small group are expected to be active; which etymologically speaking is almost a self-contradiction, but it is nevertheless true that although people are being fed into a system which looks like a medical system, they are expected to learn that the patient role is not the appropriate one for them to play. There is reason to believe that the small groups play an important part in facilitating this learning, and that they do this by the usual mechanisms of social reinforcement, i.e. people are rewarded, they win social approval, to the extent to which they do not behave like patients; for example, it is a 'good' thing, which is duly practised and encouraged, to bring your problems to the group, which means seeking a solution within a social setting, and a 'bad' thing to take your problem to a doctor, which means seeking a solution within a medical setting.

Within the field of treatment philosophies, then, Grendon can be seen to have its clearest affiliations with the therapeutic community philosophy. It may be additionally helpful to look at it within a wider social context, and here it is illuminating to look at Robertson's[6] conceptualisation in terms of changes in value systems, and the relationship of these developments to penal policy. Robertson sees emerging a value system called the 'experimental value system'. This is seen as a kind of dialectical solution of two contrasting preceding value systems, the protestant and the permissive. The protestant value system, which is easily seen to correspond with Victorian penal practice, is said to be characterised by a high moralistic tone, the concept of individual responsibility, the rationality of human behaviour, and the individual capacity for self-improvement. The permissive value system is seen as the antithesis in the dialectical conflict, and is considered to be highly coloured by Freudian thinking. Hence, as opposed to the ideas of rationality and responsibility, behaviour is seen as dominated by unconscious irrational impulses, and, treatment-wise, the freedom to act out supersedes the ideas of constraint and discipline. The goal of treatment is seen as the achievement of an internal equilibrium within the individual. The hypothesised emergent experimental value system is seen as resolving the tension between the two previous conflicting value systems. It incorporates the optimistic protestant assumption of the rationality and reformability of man, and also the humanism of the permissive value system. It is said to repair a major defect of the permissive value system, its lack of a moral imperative, which was of course very prominent in the protestant value system. Recognition of a moral imperative means of course, recognition of an individual's relationship to other people, to his social context. In a permissive psychodynamically orientated system, the treatment emphasis is on putting things right within the individual; in the emerging experimental value system the emphasis is on the improved functioning of the individual within the social context, and the relevance of group and community directed therapy to this kind of objective is easily seen. It might be suggested that, in relation to treatment of criminal behaviour, the protestant value system is associated with a moralistic model; the permissive with a medical model (this suggestion is made with a certain amount of hesitation); and the experimental system with a social psychological model. In terms of this conceptualisation, the present author sees most of the Grendon features in an area between two value systems, the permissive and the experimental; on the one hand there is plenty of permissiveness, acting out, and lip-service to psycho-dynamic formulations; on the other hand, the strongest emphasis is on relating to other people, functioning in a social context. But this latter feature includes plenty of moral pressure, including defining the limits of the treatment situation, which could well be seen as a 'protestant' characteristic having a functional value and not simply surviving as a vestigial anachronism.

This stressing of where Grendon stands is especially relevant to the topic of this chapter because of two points:

(a) Changes in value systems impose strains on front-line staff, in this case the prison officers;
(b) Theoretically, it is possible that group work could help reduce these strains.

To deal with the first point — value systems may change, but it is unrealistic to imagine that the changes will be accepted with equal alacrity at every social level (or, which amounts to much the same thing here, at every level within the hierarchical structure of an institution such as a prison). They are accepted with the most intensity by those who hear most about them, which in effect means those who are most exposed to the educational environments where such ideas are floated; in short, to those who are most educated. In practical terms, within a prison setting, this means people like progressive-minded governors, social workers, psychologists, doctors, etc.; only minimally will it involve prison officers. There is thus scope for a dangerous divergence of values. In a traditional prison system there is probably little difference in values between the management and the disciplinary staff (analogously one would expect, despite the wide social gaps, little difference in essential values between the traditional sergeant-major and the traditional commanding officer). But it is very clear that the permissive and experimental value systems have been accepted, insofar as they have been accepted, with very much more enthusiasm amongst prison professional and managerial staff than they have amongst the front-line staff. The danger here is that values which are accepted by the management are received with much less enthusiasm, or are rejected by, the front-line staff — which means, in effect, that they are not implemented at all except in a ritualistic and/or derisory fashion. Much of the Grendon management's efforts is therefore directed to getting front-line staff to see something worthwhile in values which start out by being more or less exclusively management values.

More will be said of this below, but in the meantime we must turn to our second point, that group work might do something to lessen the risks of conflict in this situation. Briefly, it could be argued that it gives a therapeutic task to disciplinary staff, and through this a greater sense of involvement with the institution's official ideology. Some empirical evidence for this will be cited below.

It would appear from the above discussion that Grendon has two sets of aims, which may be called the psychological and the sociological. By psychological we mean the changes which are presumed to denote some kind of betterment in the inmates, and here we are really talking about the primary task of the institution. If the imports to the system are highly recidivist criminals, the conversion process something called psychotherapy, then the exports are individuals who are in some way improved by the conversion process. But improved in what way? Since the intake is described as very criminal, and since one of the axioms of the establishment — an axiom because nobody considers it necessary to question it, at any rate within the context of institutional activity — is that criminality is undesirable, it follows that a cessation of criminality, if not synonymous with, would at least be a powerful indicator of improvement. Therefore, the primary task of the institution is to secure a reduction in criminal behaviour, something which would not have occurred if the people concerned had not come to Grendon; which means, in effect, that success in the primary task is measured by the negative criterion of the person's name not reappearing in the criminal statistics. This, to be sure, is not the usual way in which success in psychotherapy is assessed, but it is the most publicly ascertainable criterion of improvement in social functioning, and no matter how 'dynamically' success in psychotherapy may be defined, in the final analysis few will be convinced that it has taken place unless some operational definition of success is forthcoming. The snag is that success as indicated by the above criterion, if it occurs at all, cannot be known to have occurred until a long time has elapsed after the inmate has left the institution, and in practice there is a strong temptation to define success in terms of improved interpersonal functioning within the institution, and indeed to invest such improvement with the status of an aim of the system. Such interim satisfaction could be justified, or rather rationalised, by the assumption of transferability referred to above. In actual fact it is very tempting for the staff not to look that far ahead, but to think of such intra-institutional improvement as an end in itself. This is really saying two things: firstly, that although the institution is geared to the inmate's rehabilitation, the staff have got their own psychological needs, and secondly that Grendon, like any other institution, is liable to develop its own functional autonomy, and an act of self-discipline is needed not to lose sight of the primary task.

This leads straight on to its sociological aims. Here we refer to the endeavours to create a certain kind of culture based on assumptions very different from those of the traditional prison culture. Again, it is tempting to regard the creation of such a culture — which has been at least partially achieved — as an aim in itself; indeed, it could be argued that such a procedure is justified, in other words that to create a more humane and civilised prison is intrinsically a desirable aim, and would be justified even if no reduction in subsequent criminality could be demonstrated. This, however, invokes the kind of value judgement which is beyond the scope of this chapter. For the moment attention must be confined to the connection between small group work and (a) the psychological improvement of the individual, and (b) the creation of a particular kind of institutional ethos.

How the Regime Operates

First, however, a word about the administrative arrangements which purport to facilitate the above aims.

The prison population is housed in five wings, three adult and two boys (17–21): each wing is a therapeutic unit, with its own 'territory' as regards living and recreational areas. Most of the official and a good deal of the unofficial therapeutic activity goes on in the wings. A wing is supervised by one or two therapists (i.e. doctor or psychologist), who are responsible for their own case load, also for the wing management. Personnel-wise, apart from therapist(s), a wing consists of 40–50 inmates, 10–12 uniformed prison officers, headed by a Principal Officer. Each wing can call on the services of extra-wing agencies such as Welfare Officer and P.S.W. The most thorough-going milieu therapy regime exists in one of the boys' wings on which community and small group meetings are held daily — the other boys' wing is a paternalist regime, where psychotherapy is exclusively individual. Boys are allocated to the two wings on a random basis, for it is hoped eventually to do a follow-up study to test the efficiency of the two systems.

The adult wings are also organised on milieu therapy lines, but not to the same extent as the boys' wing described above — community meetings are held three times a week and small group meetings twice. (N.B. all inmates and all members of wing staff are expected to attend the community meetings.)

With the exception of the paternalist boys' wing population, all inmates are members of a small group. Some of these groups are conducted by prison officers. As was said above, such officer-conducted groups represent the characteristic unit of Grendon treatment. Furthermore, the prison officers, as front-line staff, have the largest number of face-to-face contacts with inmates, and at Grendon such contacts need to be very different from the discipline-orientated officer–inmate contacts which would be appropriate in a more conventional penal set-up. One way or another, therefore, the officer–inmate relationship is fundamental to the Grendon system, and it is a relationship based on reduction of social distance, which goes very much against the grain of both the prison officer and prison inmate culture; in a traditional prison, officers and inmates who go too far towards reducing the distance are liable to be regarded with suspicion by their respective groups.

The officer's role at Grendon, although it may offer advantages in the form of greater job satisfaction, is not necessarily a comfortable one. In the first place there is plenty of scope for confusion around the question; where to draw the boundaries of therapy, beyond which a disciplinary role becomes once more appropriate. Secondly, it is not pleasant to be exposed to the manipulation of psychopaths given an unwanted freedom to act out, all for the sake of a value system which is not necessarily the officers' own. It can readily be seen that there are plenty of possibilities for the emergence of many sorts of negative feelings. To cope with this the institution has to think in terms of staff training, on-going staff support, and in the case of officer group workers the question needs to be asked: what aspects of the institution's structure help to make the officers' group work meaningful?

Initiatory Training

Initiatory training can be seen as an attempt at desensitisation. It is known that there is a good deal in the Grendon system that is likely to arouse anxiety in the newly arrived—and often newly recruited—prison officer. Initiatory training, amongst other things, aims both to tell him about this and to offer as much reassurance as is possible within the limitations of a training course.

Training comes in two parts. The first part is of primarily informational content. The newcomer is told both about the things that go on at Grendon and the theory on which it is based. A week's intensive course involves such topics as: the theory of the therapeutic community, the place of small group work, psychiatric terminology, psychological tests, addiction, developmental factors, etc. Leading figures in the institution are called in to lecture and course members are encouraged to criticise freely (there is a generous time allowance for discussion) the intention being to minimise feelings of hierarchical consciousness by encouraging a questioning attitude towards the institution 'experts'. Although the course is officially about things, a good deal of time is, in fact, spent in talking about feelings. A questionnaire devised by the present author has revealed that the course is felt by the students to be very useful, and, perhaps significantly, the most useful aspect is not so much the formal subject matter as the opportunities for discussion and airing of feelings. Typical comments are that they have got to 'know' figures in the institutional hierarchy who had formerly been seen as distant. For officers who are new to the prison service the instruction course is followed by a year's supervision, including training tutorials by an officially designated training Chief Officer.

The second part is another week's course (to be attended by all newly joined staff, not just basic grade junior officers), consisting mainly of group work sessions with a psychologist acting as group leader, pointing out what is going on in terms of interactions between members, and endeavouring to increase both self-awareness and sensitivity in interpersonal relationships. The course is terminated by a review session in which it is hoped that members will see the relevance of what has been learnt to what goes on in the work situation; in effect, that they will see what has gone on in the course as a microcosm of institutional relationships. Invariably, problems of authority are thrown up, the most recurrent being that authority is uncaring, arbitrary and insensitive to the staff's status anxieties. Relationships downwards, i.e. with inmates, are as great a pre-occupation, and indeed tend to get blurred with authority difficulties, the most frequent fantasy being that authority, as personified by psychiatrists, is linked in an unholy alliance with inmates to make life difficult for the officer. Authority cares about the prisoner but doesn't care about the prison officer.

Originally, the group work course, as it has come to be called, was meant to be a training only for those officers who had volunteered to conduct groups. However, it has now been made obligatory for all newly joined staff irrespective of grade; the reasoning being that, whether or not they actually conduct groups, people have to interact continually with other people, across status barriers, and largely without the usual rank safeguards which elsewhere would serve as a protection. It is difficult to see how they could do this without some awareness, however dim, of interpersonal processes. In any case, everyone at Grendon deals with inmates who are on groups, and if only for that reason they should know what it feels like to be on a group (it might, for example, enable them the better to understand the mechanisms of resistance).

Officers who wish to undertake group work make this known to the therapist of their wing; if he thinks they are suitable he will allocate them to a group, either in sole charge, or as a joint leader with a more experienced officer; a new officer may also partner a doctor or psychologist as group leader. It should be made clear at this point that the groups are wing based, that is to say the inmate members, and the group leaders, are all members of the same wing therapy unit.

Support for Group Workers

Once officers are put in charge of groups, the problem arises of on-going support for these leaders, since they are likely to flounder without such support (and often do even with it). This is formally provided for in the institution's time-table by two weekly sessions in charge of a psychologist. These sessions cut across wing boundaries, in that they are attended by group leaders from all wings. Broadly speaking it could be said that these sessions offer support in two ways:

(a) TECHNIQUES

Frequently members come along with specific problems arising from difficulties that have arisen in their group leadership, and look to their colleagues to offer advice. Typical problems are the member who talks too much, the member who talks too little, group escapist behaviour, attempts to lead the group back to an anti-social culture, attempts by 'intellectuals' to lead the group, members dodging any significant discussion of their problems, threats of violence, refusal to attend group sessions, verbal intimidation, and so on. The usual pattern is that the member states his problem, other members attempt to interpret what is going on in his group, and suggest to him how he might deal with it. In theory at least this is the pattern — but the group workers' group is not itself immune from group phenomena; its task might be a technical advisory one, but it might avoid the task and become swamped by its own feelings; for example, instead of giving their colleague the help he ostensibly asks for, they might instead vent a good deal of verbal aggression against the psychiatrist (who, of course, is not present) who is seen as not giving enough support to the troubled officer. In such instances, the psychologist in charge of the group will point out what he thinks is happening to them, and hope that this will be a piece of relevant learning.

(b) FEELING

There is not a well defined dividing line between 'technical' and 'feeling' support, and quite obviously the officer who brings a technical problem to the group is also saying that he is feeling something about his inability to deal with the problem unaided. Nevertheless, it is possible to make a distinction. It is possible to distinguish the situation when the support group is considering a technical problem on Mr. X's group, from that in which the session is about Mr. X's feelings about his group (but of course it not infrequently happens that the former turns into the latter). A wide range of feelings may be expressed, but for the most part feelings operate around the officer's specialism as a group leader. This specialism is generally highly prized, and often overjealously guarded; fears of impotence and de-skilling are proprtionately high. The fear of de-skilling can come from above, or below, or both. From below, there are the feelings of inadequacy when the officer is unable to get the group to work; the group de-skills him by avoiding its therapeutic task, or by throwing up a leader with whom he is unable to compete (for example, an intellectualiser with a verbal and educational level higher than that of the average prison officer). From above he may feel himself de-skilled by the wing therapist who does not give him sufficient help in dealing with difficult group members, or belittles his skill by appearing indifferent to the group's activities, or does not call on the group officer's expertise in important areas of decision. The task of the support group then is, as its name implies, to provide on-going learning for the group workers, and the field of such learning has come to include not only their functioning as group leaders, but the whole question of their functioning within the institution. It does not follow that the task is at all times being effectively carried out; there are two groups of factors with impede the task:

External: i.e. The various pressures that may prevent members from turning up at the group meetings; there is competition between the demand that attendance should be a priority, and the demand that essential services must be adequately manned in other parts of the institution, and vigilance is needed to maintain a high level priority for group workers' time. The position at Grendon in this respect is probably more satisfactory than at other prisons practising group work, but it would be ostrich-like to deny that there is tension between the institution's primary task, and institutional sub-systems which have a vested interest in competing claims on staff time. In short, at Grendon as in other social organisations, there is a gap between the official ethos and the practices of sub-groups with somewhat different aims.

Internal: This group is as prone as any other group to display the usual mechanisms whereby groups avoid their officially designated task.

Advanced Training

Another form of on-going training is what has come to be known as the advanced (as opposed to the initiatory) group work course. This is very much 'better' than previous forms of training. To it are called all group workers—not just officers—who have accumulated some experience. The course is of 5 days' duration and comprises:

(a) SMALL GROUP WORK

In these sessions each member in turn assumes the role of group leader, and is subsequently discussed and criticised for the competence with which he has handled the session, the criterion being how well he has been able to make the group more aware of what is happening within itself. In this context an increased awareness means a greater sensitivity to inter-personal relationships and to group processes. The exercise is an attempt to see how well the group leader can perceive these events and bring home his perceptions to the group. (In their training sessions, incidentally, officers are presented with a non-directive model of group leadership with emphasis on work by members, and on the elucidation by the leader of inter-personal relationships in the here and now. The function of the leader is shown to be that of somebody who helps the group to work out for itself what is happening, rather than that of someone who advises, teaches, preaches, etc. It would appear from the 'exercises' described above that this model is not universally easy to assimilate. There seems to be a continuum from the non-directive, elucidatory kind of leader to the paternalist who directs and gives 'good advice'.)

(b) LARGE GROUP WORK

The total course membership is about 20, and this constitutes the large group. Two psychologists and a doctor act as consultants. The task is to see what happens in a large group—typical phenomena observed are the emergence of myths, particularly about the more or less nefarious activities of authority, the formation of sub-groups, the rise and fall of individuals within the group, scapegoating. The hope is that the large group experience is relevant: relevant, that is, within the context of their working lives in the institution they will be going back to after the course. The hope is that it increases their understanding of institutional phenomena and their own reactions to them, also perhaps their empathy for understanding inmates' reactions to institutional pressures.

(c) INTER-GROUP EXERCISES

Here members are expected to form groups amongst themselves, with the objective of studying relationships between groups. The point of including these exercises is to attempt to understand institutional dynamics by seeing the prison as an inter-group situation. Both the inmate and the staff populations are differentiated into sub-groups, on the basis of roles and status. Groups interact with each other, set up barriers against each other, generate myths about each other, have anxieties about each other. The course endeavours to reproduce a microcosmic model of the institution. Significantly, it is the inter-group exercises which are felt by members to be the 'hottest' part of the course.

At the end of the course a 're-entry' session is held, in which the attempt is made to show the relevance of the course events to the back-at-work situation; but one gets the impression that this has been perceived well before the end of the course.

The Small Group and the Institutional Ethos

On-going support for small-group work involves more than the provision of formal training courses, important though this is (and indeed it might be regretted that more time is not allocated for such training). More fundamentally it involves, or should involve, the setting up of the kind of management structure where the role of the group worker becomes meaningful. Group counselling—to use the term which the Prison Department has imported from the Californian Department of Correction*—is not peculiar, or original, to Grendon. It takes place, or has taken place, in several other penal institutions in this country. It has not always caught on, and it is felt that one reason for this is that it has been an excrescence grafted on to a traditionally authoritarian organisation, whereas it is difficult to see how it could function in any but a comparatively libertarian system in which the usual hierarchical social distances have been reduced. What is needed is the kind of structure which can receive and treat as useful the communications fed into it by the counselling officers. Group leadership is presumably like any other piece of behaviour in that it will continue only if it is reinforced. No officer is compelled to take a group, so it must be assumed that those who do, do so because they feel there is something in it for them.

What is this something? This author's impression is that it is a satisfaction of status needs, arising from the feeling of doing a job which has some point in terms of the institution's primary task. If this need is not satisfied the activity is not reinforced and will cease—as indeed has happened in some cases, either because the officer's need was too strong to be satisfied, or because there really was a failure of reinforcement due to faults in the structure. To be precise, reinforcement would come from the group officer feeling that he is a person of some consequence, who knows something important, and should be listened to when he communicates it. Whether or not this satisfactory state of affairs has

---

*Dr. Norman Fenton introduced Group Counselling in California in 1944 in an attempt to break down barriers between inmates and prison staff. It aimed to change the structure of establishments by changing the quality of relationships. Fenton explains his concepts in several handbooks (Fenton 7, 8). In 1958 Group Counselling was introduced into the British prison service.

been fully achieved at Grendon, it obviously cannot be if the group transactions remain an encapsulated activity. This would mean that the boundary of the group became a barrier. This could happen if the officer felt that his status needs were better served by adapting a quasi-medical attitude of confidentiality about 'his' group's activities. Also, if management created a barrier between its functions and those of the group counsellors resulting in the latter being sealed off from the wider treatment field. By and large this does not happen at Grendon, and indeed, has no business to happen in an institution whose official ideology is that everybody in the community is a potential treatment agent (the fact that it happens at all shows the extent to which there is still a hangover from different sets of assumptions, both penal and medical).

It is possible to see over the years a continuous increase in the status of the group officer and in the prestige of the small group. Formerly, when an important decision needed to be made about an inmate the automatic question was 'What does the therapist think?'. Now it is almost as automatic to ask 'What does the group officer think?' and even when the question is first put to the therapist, it is unlikely that he would answer without consulting the group officer. The group officer's opinion is sought on a wide range of instances, from the comparatively minor, such as whether the inmate should be allowed to change his labour, to the major issue whether an inmate's treatment should be terminated by his 'expulsion' from Grendon. A group officer in turn is most unlikely to make an *ex cathedra* pronouncement on an issue of importance—he would himself consult with the group. This decision making becomes a process in which therapist, group officer and group members participate. No pretence can be made that they are equal participants—the therapist has the ultimate responsibility and so must reserve a right of veto; and it becomes a delicate managerial problem to get this point accepted without the riposte from inmates and officers 'it makes no difference what we say, the therapist will always have the last word'. The difference from the traditional authoritarian model is not, of course, the abandonment by management of responsibility, but in the involvement of the various levels in decision making, with greater opportunities for them to influence or even to pressurise management.

Increasingly, group officers are seen as agents for facilitating contact between the inmates on their groups and the outside world. When an inmate needs to go out on escort for some stressful purpose, e.g. to be interviewed for a job, look for lodgings, mend relationships with his family, it is his group officer who takes him, and may even participate in difficult family situations. Increasingly, ex-inmates write to and visit their former group officers, and are visited by them (a process which has been developed furthest with the young offenders): no statistics are available, but the impression is that ex-inmate contacts with group officers are much more frequent than with therapists.

It appears then that Grendon has at least avoided the pitfall of letting the small group work develop into an encapsulated ritual with little more than a public relations value; and that by and large, group officers feel that they are making an important contribution. The group officer is a significant and helpful figure in the inmate's institutional life, and this relationship is liable to continue after his institutional life is over. It should not be imagined that it is only group counselling officers who enter the treatment field and thereby abandon a purely custodial role; as well as the various meetings described above, there are frequent wing staff meetings which provide a forum for exchange between therapist and all wing staff, whether or not they are group leaders. But a recent administrative re-shuffle has greatly increased the proportion of wing officers who conduct groups.

Now it has to be asked what the small group work does to the inmates, whose behaviour must be the final criterion for judging the whole system. This question is not easy to answer. Certainly, the Grendon social atmosphere is very different from that of any other penal establishment in this country, being characterised by a relaxed and less formalised pattern of relationships right the way up the hierarchy. Specifically, this is most noticeable in the officer–inmate relationship, and statistically it can be seen in the fact that at Grendon the incidence of disciplinary reports is much less than that of establishments with similar populations—or indeed of the same population when they were at other prisons; the reason for this is not necessarily that the inmates behave any better, but that the officers have learnt different ways of coping with their behaviour. But it is not possible to say that the small group work has produced this result; it has been shown that the group work is embedded in a system which is congenial to it. If the system does indeed produce something which is different from, say, Dartmoor or Pentonville, it can only be guesswork how much of this has been brought about by any one feature such as the small groups, and this caveat must be borne in mind in the following discussion.

Impressionistically, it seems that pressures come from groups for inmates to behave, or at least to verbalise, in ways that conform more to the values of conventional society than to those of the criminal sub-groups; or if you like, to verbalise the kind of things that therapists would tend to cite as changes for the better in a psychopathic population—e.g. an insistence on accepting the fact of authority, or adopting realistic rather than fantasy goals, or holding less egocentric attitudes, etc. (This is not always distastefully breast-beating although it often is.) Reality confrontation is a favourite slogan of milieu therapy theorists, and it would appear that, at any rate at the verbal level, small group work facilitates this, if only because whilst it may be easy to hoodwink a middle-class therapist, it is much harder to 'con' one's own peers. If reality confrontation does occur, it appears to do so via pressure from peer group members, and it may be that a behaviourist social reinforcement model is the most appropriate for understanding this. Members win approval from their peers if they say certain things rather than others, and since approval of their peers is something they value, the likelihood of their saying these things is increased; there is nothing particularly startling in this. What is surprising is that the group values which confront the new members, and which he is pressurised to introject, are no different from the values which previous experience has led him to expect from his peers. Such changes in a conventionally acceptable direction are not entirely confined—although they often are—to the verbal level. Behavioural changes also occur—violent people refrain from hitting others, workshy people become more industrious, rebellious people become more reasonable with authority figures, etc. (it depends entirely on one's value orientation whether such changes are considered 'desirable').

Whether or not through the causative agency of the small groups a culture has been created different from the conventional prison culture, and it might be interesting to look at this culture via the beliefs which are considered to be out of date.

Firstly, there is the belief in the wickedness of prison officers, or at least in the necessity to avoid close relationships with them. In the traditional prison the inmate and custodial populations view each other with mutual suspicion, and it seems quite likely that hostile acts committed by each group against the other are rather like the realisation of self-fulfilling prophecies. At Grendon there is a marked diminution—although not complete absence—of the expectation that the other side will act malevolently. Clearly, in view of the behaviour of the group officers described above, it is difficult to maintain a belief in the external malevolence of authority. Inmates who, at large or small group meetings, attempt to use the group as a weapon against institutional authority, do not usually succeed. They are not told that it is *wrong* to attack staff—this would be disturbingly virtuous—but it is usually conveyed that the slogan 'all screws are bastards' is very much last year's model, a pattern of behaviour that has been outmoded; in *this* society we operate on somewhat different assumptions.

Also there is from the officer's side a movement away from traditional prison culture assumptions, and towards more normal relationships with inmates. It cannot be assumed that this movement matches the inmate movement in extent. It must be remembered that the inmates have a good deal to gain from reductions in social distances, since it tends to make their imprisonment so much more comfortable. The officers too may have a lot to gain, but for them such a reduction is not always immediately comfortable. And in both officer and inmate populations there are sub-cultures very much opposed to the official culture. Optimistically, the institution assumes that it can either convert or contain these elements. What is immediately relevant is that officers committed to group work have moved markedly further towards the new pattern of inmate/officer relationship.

Another obsolescent belief is the inmate taboo on 'grassing'—i.e. tale-bearing. Traditionally, grassing is a serious misdemeanour against the inmate culture, and can result in severe manhandling of the culprit. The essence of grassing is to inform authority of the misdeeds of one's fellow inmates, it is in fact a severe limitation of the communications which are allowed across the staff-inmate boundary. Clearly, it is the kind of rule which is incompatible with group work, since so much of the group's business is about precisely those bits of behaviour which in other contexts it would be grassing to let authority know about; and, of course, authority is present in the person of the group officer. The no-grassing rule could have effectively stifled any significant group work. In practice, the group work has abolished the no-grassing rule. An inmate who invokes the no-grassing rule to escape group pressures is told, often very explicitly, that he is invoking something which is an archaism.

Lastly, it is worth noting that group work erodes, and of course makes out of date, the deep-rooted inmate assumption that other inmates are not to be trusted. This is indeed self-evident, since if this assumption had not withered away there would be no group work worth writing about. On the group, members reveal themselves in the presence of each other in a way which would be considered, to say the least, highly unwise in a traditional prison where the official belief is that no good can come from letting fellow-inmates know one's business. For example, in the prisoner hierarchy the offender against children holds the lowest of places and is lucky to escape physical maltreatment. At Grendon it is not uncommon for such people to make public statements of their offences, either on large or small groups. To the outsider such 'confessions' may seem contrived and distasteful, and in fact, often are. They may have little therapeutic value for the individual, but they do have a symbolic value; it demonstrates the person's belief that he is now in a culture where he will not be beaten up for offending against children, and may indeed be socially rewarded for having made the admission.

Next, it must be asked how knowledge of group processes is available. It is an important question because the fact that some such knowledge is available means that the groups are not closed systems. It is disseminated through various feedback arrangements:

Communication from group counsellor to the appropriate therapist.
Communication from the counsellor to his colleagues on the wing unit.
Most important of all, communication from group members to their fellow-inmates at the Wing Community Meetings.

Groups, therefore, operate as facilitators of communication within the institution, in other words they have an organisational significance, since no organisation, libertarian or authoritarian, can function without adequate communication. It might be said that they were being therapeutic at one degree removed—it may be that the transactions of the groups are themselves therapeutic, but beyond this it could be said that by improving communications they assist in the primary task of the institution which is by definition therapeutic (although the claim that groups, or any other aspect of the system, are therapeutic could only be finally established if it could be shown that the institution carries out its primary task by some criteria *other* than behaviour within the institution). The fact that communication takes place across group boundaries shows that there has been a breakdown in the concept of group confidentiality, and the fact that groups have developed from closed systems into facilitators of communication, are very important facts both about the history of the groups themselves and of the system generally. Confidentiality at Grendon has not disappeared—there is some variation between the wings—but it has been severely eroded; for example, pairing relationships, whether between patient and patient or patient and doctor, are frowned on. Confidentiality of group proceedings was in the first instance assumed and insisted on, and was a sizeable obstacle to the development of a therapeutic community because of the impediment to free-flowing communications; it could, for example, stop any feed-back from small groups to community meetings, and thus lead to the trivialisation of the latter's proceedings. The ending of confidentiality may be an interesting pointer of the transition from medical to social psychological model, if it is remembered that confidentiality is an important element of the doctor–patient social contract. (It may be asked why ever the idea of confidentiality should have been assumed in the first place; it seems rather analogous to the first railway carriages being shaped like the road coaches they superseded. There was no functional value in such a shape but nobody at that stage could imagine any other shape for vehicles to be.)

The diminution of confidentiality has been and still is resisted, and it is interesting to look at the motives for such resistance. On the part of the inmates it is bound up with the difficulty of extending the area of trust. Inmate–inmate distrust may be modified to the extent that individuals will reveal themselves on small groups. But a further effort is needed before it can be expected that such communications will be revealed to a far wider audience.

With the officers, one suspects that it is part of the anxiety over de-skilling mentioned above. The officer who successfully conducts a group perceives what he has carved out as an important role for himself; the exclusive relationship with the group becomes an important need for him; to share his communications with persons outside the group represents a reduction of his own territory.

Evaluation

In conclusion, the problems must be faced as to how the effect of group work at Grendon can be evaluated.

Firstly, it will be clear from the above account that one of the administrative problems at Grendon is to help the custodial staff feel a sense of identification with the institution's values. It should perhaps be made clear that here is a situation somewhat different from management training in other spheres. In situations where, to put it simply, upper management provides training for middle or junior management, it can probably be assumed that there is an identity of values between those being trained and those providing training. In the penal setting this cannot be assumed and indeed the function of training may well be to facilitate such an identity. In this context, it is worth considering group work as a factor in helping the desired processes. Marcus,[9] in a study of correlates of attitude to group work, found that officers who believed in small group work tended to hold certain attitudes consistent with the institution's philosophy. These can be summed up as (a) a wish to reduce social distances between themselves and inmates, (b) a feeling that there was not a wide social distance between themselves and professional staff, and (c) an agreement with the procedures and activities usually associated with milieu therapy; but it cannot be assumed that conducting small groups has *caused* the officers to feel this way, it seems more likely that officers interested in conducting groups would tend to hold opinions which might loosely be called liberal or therapy orientated, but it can at any rate be claimed that the holding of pro-group attitudes goes with certain opinions that makes more feasible the operation of this sort of regime.

Secondly, the group work should be evaluated in terms of relationships between the inmates. It is difficult to say much here beyond the impressionistic level but a small control study has been possible in view of the fact, as mentioned above, that one boys' wing is organised on exclusively individual therapy and paternalist lines and, therefore, serves as a control with the population of boys on the milieu therapy boys' wing. Sociometric studies have been done on both populations and it seems clear that the differences are in the predicted directions. That is to say, there is a more intense level of feeling on the group orientated boys' wing. Sociograms of both popularity and unpopularity are more highly structured, indicating the feeling level of both liking and disliking is higher. By contrast, the individual therapy wing shows a lower degree of relatedness among the inmates, and a larger number of isolates, i.e. people who do not feel about others and who do not have any feelings directed towards them.

Thirdly, one might look at the area of inmates' attitudes to staff. Impressionistically, these seem very different from those obtaining in more conventional prisons. But there is no need to rely entirely on impressions.

Recently, a simple questionnaire on attitudes to imprisonment was administered both to Grendon inmates and to the inmates of a more conventional prison (Oxford).[10] In the first place, it was very clear that Grendon inmates were more contented with their conditions of imprisonment. Take for example the question:

'Is this prison better or worse than other prisons?'

The distribution of answers is as follows:*

	Oxford	Grendon
Better	22	94
Same	22	7
Worse	56	1

* All figures quoted are in percentages.

This is a very clear-cut result but not very startling — no one will be surprised to learn that prisoners prefer to be imprisoned under more, rather than less, pleasant conditions.

Of rather more interest is the fact that Grendon inmates — although by no means unanimously so — have more hope that imprisonment can do them some good.

'Can imprisonment achieve any good?'

	Oxford	Grendon
Yes	33	58
No	67	42

Most relevant to this chapter are questions relating to the desire for more normal, uninstitutionalised relationships with prison officers for example:
'Would you prefer it if officers wore plain clothes?'
(i.e. instead of uniform)

	Oxford	Grendon
Yes	38	84
No	62	16

'Would you like to have closer contact with officers?'

	Oxford	Grendon
Yes	48	80
No	52	20

Questionnaire results therefore indicate that Grendon inmates want closer relationships with prison officers, as contrasted with what appears to be the case in the more typically prison culture at Oxford. This, of course, is in line with the predictions that have been implied in this chapter.

If one says that the development of a civilised pattern of relationships within a penal setting is a worthy end in itself, then the value of Grendon is demonstrated and nothing more need be said. However, it is not likely that the institution can get off as lightly as this; the question can hardly be avoided, does the place do anything for the betterment of its population, and this in turn raises the question of the criterion of betterment that should be used. It is not likely that a better criterion can be found than the behavioural one of cessation of criminal activity, i.e. the reconviction statistics, and here evidence of validity is harder to come by. Tenuous evidence has been forthcoming that the chances of reconviction are reduced in those with comparatively light previous criminal records, but even this finding is not consistent. Control group studies do not show an overall reduction in reconviction rates for Grendon (although it is very doubtful if a fully matched control group has been found, but a more hopeful finding is that length of stay at Grendon is associated with post-release success. This means in practice that success rates, which remain fairly static for stays of up to a year, improve perceptibly after that period—even incidentally for inmates with the most severe previous criminal records). It does not appear that length of time at Grendon is itself associated with any of the factors that are found to be associated with success. What, then, is the nature of the association between length of stay and success? One would, of course, like to think they succeed *because* they spend a long time at Grendon, but all one can say is that so far the evidence remains consistent with this piece of wishful thinking. (There is, incidentally, no evidence that a lengthy sentence *per se* has a beneficial effect on success rates.) If being at Grendon a long time is beneficial, how can this be interpreted? All one can answer at this stage is little more than a tautology—whatever therapeutic processes are set in motion by the system, they take a long time before reaching a point where they begin to affect post-institutional behaviour. But it is, perhaps, not unflattering to the treatment to discover that the more of it the better.

The above comments on evaluation apply, of course, not to small group work as an isolated entity, but to a whole institutional system. But as the whole drift of this chapter has been that group work is embedded in a system consistent with it, these quoted results should not be considered irrelevant.

This chapter is published with the permission of the Prison Department, Home Office, but the views expressed are the author's own.

References

1. East, W. N., and Hubert, W. H. de B., *Report on the Psychological Treatment of Crime*, H.M.S.O., 1939.
2. Rice, A. K., *Learning for Leadership*, Tavistock Publications, 1968.
3. Jones, M., *Social Psychiatry in Practice*, Penguin Books, 1968.
4. Barton, R., *Institutional Neurosis*, 1959.
5. Goffman, E., *Asylums*, Penguin Books, 1968.
6. Robertson, A., 'Penal Policy and Social Change', *Hum. Rel.*, 22, 1969.
7. Fenton, M., *Group Counselling*, Institute for the Study and Treatment of Delinquency, Sacramento, 1961.
8. Fenton, M., *Explorations in the Use of Group Counselling in the County Correctional Program*, Pacific Books, Palo Alto, California, 1962.
9. Marcus, B., 'Correlates of Attitudes to Group Work', *Brit. J. Crim.*, 9, 1969.
10. Newton, M., Hickey, P. and Hull, G. J., *Inmates' Attitudes to Imprisonment* (unpublished), 1972.

© 1979 B. Marcus

CHAPTER 5

Small Group Work in Relation to Management Development

BY K. B. LOW AND HAROLD BRIDGER

1. Summary of Background and Aims

To set in perspective the contemporary work with small groups being carried out in the British company of this multi-national enterprise it is necessary to understand the historical background. The training courses which have been developed during the late 1960s and early 1970s had their origin in a conference held at Eastbourne in 1962, which aimed to devise means whereby the company could secure management succession. Itself the result of earlier deliberations on this theme by directors and senior managers, the conference, in turn, became the genesis of the subsequent work with small groups, in which the idea of reviewing and renewing constitutes an integral activity.

A prime influence in the creation of this awareness for taking stock was the Chief Personnel Officer, Mr. D. G. Hutchison. Together with other managers and with members of his own function he had grown concerned over the inadequacy of the methods for training supervisors and managers to meet what were felt to be circumstances of change. The economic and social climate of the post-war years had been giving way to one influenced by new needs of people, both as consumers and as employees. Different skills were becoming necessary at work where less tolerance would be shown towards authoritarian or paternalistic styles of management. Supervisors and managers would have to understand new technologies and how they affected the workforce; they would have to acquire skills in industrial relations, in exercising authority in more complex organisations where high degrees of professional and technical expertise would be dominant. The age of mechanised production, of marketing, instead of mere selling, of computerised information systems, and of graduate recruitment as a specialist activity would demand of the supervisor and manager in the future a different set of skills and a fresh orientation.

To meet the changes brought about by these technical, social and economic forces was the principal objective of the Eastbourne Staff Development Conference.

Whilst the present intention of this chapter is not to describe in detail the working methods and results of that conference, it is germane to the later development in the company of small group work that consideration be given to the role which social science consultants exercised during that week in Eastbourne. As a result of an earlier visit to the U.S.A. to study experience there with the development of managers, the Chief Personnel Officer had recognised the value which contemporary thought in the social sciences was bringing to this question. Additionally, the company recognised the importance of the recent work carried out by the Tavistock Institute and in particular of its training conference designed in conjunction with Leicester University. Invitations to assist with the planning and running of the Eastbourne Conference were, therefore, extended to Professor M. Miles of Teachers College, Columbia University and to E. Trist and his colleagues at the Tavistock Institute. What is important here is that a precedent was being established for the role of consultant to help not only with the output task ('content') of a conference, but also with the related task of understanding how ways of working ('process') can determine output. Members of the Tavistock Institute, in particular, welcomed this opportunity to work within the U.K. sector of a multi-national company as they had seen the future developments of the concept of 'socio-technical systems'* to lie across national boundaries.

The principal aims, deriving from the Eastbourne Conference, which were to inform the nature of the subsequent work with small groups, were:

(i) To ensure through staff development, and in particular through an appraisal system, the continuity of management in a changing environment.

(ii) To develop interpersonal skills in order to gain benefit from any staff appraisal system.

(iii) To provide managers with experience of appraising and of giving feedback.

(iv) To consider the relevance of group training methods to the growth of awareness about individual behaviour and the link between this and increased group effectiveness.

From a concern to train individuals in the many interpersonal aspects of group life, the current courses represent an evolution towards a concern for managers to understand how a group functions when faced with a task. With a conscious intention to convey a sense of practicality and reality to the managers who were to attend the training courses, a title 'Practice of Management' was chosen. Although the purpose was to teach behavioural skills it was thought essential to emphasise, even in the course title, the relevance of management as an integral group process to its practical effects upon the outcome of work.

The introduction in 1963 in a U.K. industrial setting of a form of training

---

*'Socio-technical systems'. See Trist, E. L. pp. 269–82 in *The Planning of Change*, 1969, ed. Bennis Benne & Chin.

applying the findings and experience of social science, in relation to the behaviour of groups, was a rare and bold undertaking; one which needs to be acknowledged as the precursor to subsequent training developments.

2. Theoretical and Conceptual Framework

In creating the courses, reliance has not been placed exclusively on any one school of psychology but assumptions adopted emphasise self and group development and so have more in common with the work of Freud and the social anthropologists than, for example, with the experiments of the behaviourists.

For hypotheses about small group behaviour and the effects of such behaviour upon the work of organisations, much is owed to Bion. But, underlying the courses as they developed, were a number of ideas that needed to be substantiated in practice.

(i) That while a group consists of individuals, the group itself exists as an entity with an identifiable culture.

When individuals, each with his need to adapt as well as to resist, come together as a collection of people, then the group which forms develops a life of its own. It too will have the capacity both to change and to learn, as well as to resist change and to avoid work. The group, like the individual, will develop and will grow in understanding, and it will wish for both stability and movement. Recognition of this existence of a group culture, as a factor that affects the practical output of a group, is basic in these training courses. This culture characterises a group and is not predictable from acquaintance with the individuals in it. A group is, in this sense, more than the sum of its parts.

(ii) That, while the process of learning is experiential and the learners can draw lessons from a shared experience, they need the help of a trainer, or consultant, to relate these lessons to a conceptual framework, which the consultant can provide, as well as to their experiences in management in the external world.

(iii) That it is possible, through experience in a group, for an individual to modify behaviour.

The consultant, however, needs to recognise that what the learner learns grows from the learner's experience, internal state and view of reality, not from what the consultant supposes to be that state, nor from some position held or envisaged by the consultant himself. The lessons learnt by each learner will be particular to him, and so will any modification of behaviour that results. A consultant must bear these points in mind and is responsible for the method he uses to assist such learning to take place.

(iv) That it is possible for individuals, and the group as a whole, to deal simultaneously with matters of content (and so carry out a task) and with matters of process (and so become aware of internal dynamics).

This statement holds with regard to activities (i.e. to doing) and to reviewing what has been done; it is also important (see Sect. 3, Work Groups) that a balance be achieved between the less familiar need for reviewing and the more familiar need for activity. In reviewing, as in activity, there must be a balance between concern for content and concern for process.

While this emphasis on the duality of content and process (and the drawing of inferences therefrom) may not be usual, except in therapy groups, it is held relevant here to understanding the life and development both of individuals and of groups at work. This feature (the duality of content and process) above all typifies the course and differentiates it from contemporary T-groups with their strictly inter-personal flavour.

(v) Tasks (as opposed to self analysis) which a group can carry out are valuable as vehicles for learning about process.

Used thus, they are a feature common to Adair and Coverdale and these courses. A difference, however, between these Practice of Management Courses and the Adair and Coverdale approaches, which all employ exercises, is that in the last two they are introduced by the training staff, while the first relies for tasks on discussion topics (such as people's motivation at work or problems of communication between Departments) brought by course participants. Concern in these courses, it must be repeated, is not simply with the content, i.e. the managerial problems that are discussed, but also to learn about the process, which has such a vital bearing upon such discussion. The dual task is, in essence, to develop awareness about process in the group and its relationship to content.

(vi) That, as in psychoanalysis, what remains unexpressed, even hidden, can be vital for the elucidation of why certain actions take place.

It is important to understand not only the influence of 'hidden agenda' in groups, but also that, though the consequent self-knowledge may be frustrating or even painful, individuals and groups have a capacity for resilience and for making changes; in other words, for learning. Only with the sanction of the members is concern about personal feelings and emotion, whether expressed verbally or in other ways, explored by the group and then only if therein there seems to be a key to an increase in knowledge about what is happening in the group.

(vii) That roles are distributed and sanctioned by the group according to the requirements of any particular situation.

The concept of role in group life, and in particular the situational aspect of leadership within the group is of basic importance. Reference has been made to the role of consultant as teacher, whose responsibility is to assist a work group in its learning task. At the outset of a course, only the consultant is clearly identified as having a role. Participants' expectations, based on other experiences of teacher or executive, are frustrated and they face a problem of authority and power. This problem turns out to be difficult to resolve; one in which, in Bion's phrase, the dependency needs of the group start to manifest themselves. It takes time for a group to discover that a consultant's leadership function relates solely to the task of learning about group behaviour.

Early in the course, when tackling what it perceives as the content of its task, i.e. those discussion topics that members have brought with them, a group begins to test, albeit unconsciously, its internal capacities for leadership. It soon recognises that no lead on this content will be given by the assumed authority (the consultant) and that the way by which the group organises itself to hold a discussion will be for itself to decide. (Such a process can become one of the early subjects for comment and observation by the consultant, against whom a certain resentment may be felt—because he is perceived as failing to give the sort of lead normally expected from one in such a clearly identified role.) As the discussion ranges over a variety of managerial topics, opportunities arise for now one, now another, member to take a leadership role, either in relation to content or to process.

The group is customarily thought of as a leaderless group, a description valid only in the sense that no one has been formally appointed Chairman to give direction to the discussions. Aided by the consultant, the group can become aware of how roles are shared between its members, according to the group's needs at any stage in its development. To be effective, a group must devote its energies and resources, and especially its leadership capacities, to whatever task is in hand. But, equally, there arise certain occasions when, at its peril, it would ignore its 'maintenance' requirements, which might be, for instance, the physical conditions under which they work, or questions of priorities in what they are doing, or uncertainties about states within the group. A group, were it to ignore such aspects of its life, could be in danger of ceasing to exist as a group capable of work. So, as it develops and as it recognises its own internal strengths and weaknesses, a group can learn to balance its content tasks with its process tasks in order to be an effective unit.

The roles associated with this need for group maintenance are not simply to do with its creature comforts; they are often vital ones in relation to particular behaviour of individuals, and are seen as not the sole prerogative of any chairman, whom the group may have wishes to elect. Thus, it emerges that through the recognition and sharing of appropriate skills for different roles, a group can develop its effectiveness. What becomes valued is the ability to understand different behaviour; not simply the judgment of behaviour, to be labelled good or bad in some absolute sense, but the acknowledgement of the appropriateness or inappropriateness of actions, dependent upon the group's situational requirements. The silent, reflective, perhaps reticent member of a group can thus be a resource equally with the voluble, bold, self-confident member. Each can be helped, and the group as a whole, too, to understand how their capacities can have relevance.

(viii) That skills in performance appraisal and in giving feed-back are improved by experience gained in groups.

It will be recalled that, initially, this type of training had as one of its principal objectives the improvement of feedback skills in the carrying out of performance appraisal. In their work groups participants, particularly when engaged in their dual content and process tasks, experience what is involved in giving and taking comments about each other and about the group. They can then see the effect, within the group, of observations that are non-judgmental in character and can compare them with any intended as judgments or evaluations.

(ix) That a group, as a 'temporary system' for the purpose of learning, can enable individuals to transfer insights to other situations.

It can be too costly in human terms for awareness to develop only through the medium of operational activity. Managers, like Army officers, need to take risks — all learning involves some degree of risk taking — preferably where survival is not at stake and where support from colleagues can assist one to learn. (There seems to be a relationship here to military ideas, and presumably to Adair's Action and Leadership theories.) To make another comparison, this time with Marcus, it is disturbing for managers and prisoners alike if the values they meet in group work are incompatible with those they meet outside the group.

A Practice of Management course constitutes, in essence, a temporary system in which learning about group behaviour can take place without the kind of inhibitions and pressures normally present for a manager at his place of work. If a first necessary step towards the solution of a problem is the development of awareness of its existence, and if insights about behaviour, as well as about the objective nature of a problem, can be gained through exposure in discussion at 'off-centre' activities like a course, then the relevance of such a temporary system may be seen to the study of organisation as a whole. To learn in this way about the interaction between a group's content work and its process can lead to attempts to examine in a similar way problems located in the laboratory, the office or the factory. Indeed, as will be noted later, evidence does point to the ability of some managers to make this transfer of insights about group behaviour, gained in the setting of the Practice of Management, to their own roles within their sponsoring organisation. The conditions under which such transfer is possible will be touched upon in a subsequent section of this chapter which refers to 'Organisation Development'.

3. Course Design

The most important aspect of any course design is that it should reflect the theories, values and assumptions which determine its purposes. If learning is held to be essentially a participant-centred activity, then a course aimed to create conditions whereby learning may take place must have as its central point the needs and expectations of those who have been invited. Similarly, if the role of the teacher is thought to be most constructive when it assists the discovery, through experience, of hitherto undiscovered knowledge and skills, then such a role must stem from personal authority not from mere status, together with sensitivity to the needs of others. It follows that the structure of a course about management will, above all else, be concerned to provide that essential framework within which managers may be free to accept or reject for themselves theories, concepts and ideas. The construction of this framework is, therefore, a vital factor in ensuring that learning can take place, equally with the selection of people to undertake staff roles.

The Practice of Management as it evolved (indeed, continues to evolve as new experiences help to shape it) has three principal phases, viz:

(i)   A Pre-course phase, to prepare for
(ii) A Residential phase (normally 1 week), followed by
(iii) A Post-course phase (including later organisation development work).

(i) PRE-COURSE PHASE

This consists of two operations. In one of these nominations are submitted from the constituent parts of the company of those managers who wish to attend, and invitations are sent by the Management Development Adviser to those nominated, setting out the purpose and indicating prior work to be done. In the other, the M.D.A. appoints the course staff and meetings between them are subsequently held 2 or 3 weeks before the residential phase.

(1) *Nominations and method of invitation*

The means by which managers decide to attend the Practice of Management have varied over time since the early series of courses which started in 1963. However, the same basic principles have applied throughout, in particular, that each participant should attend voluntarily, through the acceptance that, on the face of it at least, the course appears relevant to him. As a corollary too, each participant, after discussion with his own manager, his personnel manager, or with the organiser of the courses, i.e. the Management Development Adviser in the Central Personnel Department, must be free to withdraw at any stage. Because of its nature, the course attracts curiosity, even a desire to challenge, to test oneself against unfamiliar teaching methods (which, incidentally, has given rise to difficulties when a participant may previously have gone on record as denying or suspecting the course's validity). There has not yet been any apparent status accorded to this course in a hierarchical sense, i.e. in the sense that it is expected of a manager should he wish to get on, although among training staff it has acquired prestige. Invitations are sent on the basis that

(a) Each participant has within the scope of his management function sufficient opportunity to influence change in methods of working.
(b) The motivation to undertake fresh approaches to work and to explore problems without pre-conceptions is within the capacity of the individual managers.

(c) Course members are resilient enough to absorb conflicting pressures and can react with sensitivity.

The description of the course which is sent to those who are nominated endeavours to make clear its purpose:

> These courses (... ...) are designed to enable managers to gain, through participation in group exercises and discussion, a fresh insight into management and to derive general principles and practice from particular experiences. Course work includes such topics as interviewing; the conduct of meetings; communications; decision making. No attempt is made to teach hard and fast techniques but rather to encourage learning by participation in joint work, aided by the presentation of theoretical concepts by the course staff.

This phrasing is intended to indicate the duality of task; that through a discussion of management topics which are both valid and real, insight can not only be gained about the content of such issues, but more importantly, with the assistance of staff, to understand the relevance of process in group activity. In general, of course, managers who participate in the work groups are unfamiliar with the concept of content/process duality and will, through previous experience of discussion groups, not anticipate any other development than an airing of, perhaps even a heated argument over, the questions on an agenda, which they themselves have prepared.

By way of preparation the nominees are asked to bring, for discussion by the heterogenous 'work groups' of which they will be members, subjects which are important to them in their roles as managers. In addition they are asked to formulate a specific problem from their own managerial experience which can be discussed in detail within the homogenous 'common interest' group of which they will also be members. At one time it was possible for courses to be preceded by a half-day's briefing session, some weeks in advance. Nowadays, participants are informed, not personally but through a full description, including details of course structure and method, of the programme which is sent out in advance.

(2) *Staff selection and staff meetings*

The responsibility for inviting people to take part as staff members in the Practice of Management courses rests with the Management Development Adviser, who in turn is assisted in this task by the Tavistock Institute Consultant. From tiny beginnings when invitations were made simply on the basis of personal knowledge of an individual's competence, the increased numbers of courses has obliged the Management Development Adviser and his consultant adviser to consider the need to create a network of resources, both from within and external to the company. The criteria for the informal membership which this expanding network requires are simple:

(a) A capacity to understand the motivation of people at work in groups;
(b) Sensitivity to individual and group behaviour;
(c) Organisational roles which have credibility in a professional sense;

(d) Support from managers to do consultant work, whether with training or with operational groups; and,

(e) of course, experience as a participant in a Practice of Management course.

To avoid any feeling that participants in the courses are undergoing a selection process for becoming trainee consultants, individuals are encouraged, on later reflection about the course and its impact upon them, to appraise themselves. In this way the initiative can be left to the individual to state whether a consultant role of this type appeals. The invitation, ultimately, still remains within the prerogative of the Management Development Adviser, following discussions between the individual and himself.

As the group work on the course is a crucial element within the total course design, care is taken in the assignment of individual staff consultants to each group. Thus it is desirable that the setting up of any unnecessary inhibitions to learning be avoided by ensuring that no staff member has too close a personal or work relationship with any member of his group. Although an experienced consultant can obviously work adequately with a work group of some 8 or 9 participant managers, it has been found advantageous to include 2 staff members with each group. Sometimes these will be people of equal experience, in which case they work as co-trainers, each feeling free to intervene with comments and interpretations, thereby complementing each other's role, each knowing that if points about group behaviour slip by unnoticed by one, the other is likely to pick them up. More frequently, however, the relationship between the two staff members is that of consultant to trainee. The trainee whose role is normally described as that of observer will, along with his more experienced colleague, remain unacceptable to the group until he is felt to have earned his right to make process comments.

Staff meetings are held before the course assembles and, as with the residential phase of the course which follows, these meetings beforehand have a dual purpose. In content terms it is to determine the outline (or framework) of the week's programme; it is also in process terms to become acquainted with one another, to understand the different roles, to recognise overtly the relevance of talent and skills within the staff group to these roles, and to try to agree how the work will be shared between the staff members.

Whatever the different levels of experience among participants, it is essential to make clear from the start, so that they (the participants) may also be clear, the differences between teaching roles and administrative roles. One staff member is assigned responsibility for the running of the course, for taking decisions related to the domestic arrangements and, in general, for being seen as the person to whom questions about administration (e.g. expenses, travel arrangements, hotel facilities) can be addressed. Course members will best understand the importance of role clarity in groups if the staff themselves have made a conscious effort to distinguish their own roles, so that participants need not be in doubt when a staff member is the consultant (or teacher) in a given situation, or when, in another situation, the same person is the administrator eliciting a different sort of response.

(ii) THE RESIDENTIAL PHASE

Participants gathering at the hotel or conference centre will, despite each having received an identical course programme, bring differing expectations of what is about to take place. The order of activities in the course and the activities themselves are chosen with great care to convey not only a sense of direction and of purpose, but also a sense of unity. But precisely because it is essential to design a course with deliberate intent, it is necessary for the staff to understand the feelings of being manipulated which participants will have.

(1) *First plenary session*

At the first plenary session of the course, therefore, the staff must allow time for questions, however trivial these may seem, without creating an undue sense that time is an expandable commodity. The session attempts to be administratively brisk and clear and to explain the rationale of the course design and the roles of the staff. There is bound to exist, nevertheless, to a certain degree, a genuine sense that participants are the victims of manipulative or even devious stratagems. With the best will in the world, and despite protestations to the contrary, the staff may fail to convince that such is not their intention.

The course is frequently described as unstructured, not because a basic framework is lacking, but because it starts from the learner's questions, rather than from the teachers' answers. Exploration of problems about managing, about group behaviour, starts with discussion between participants, so that their differing or similar experiences may be brought into the open, before any inferences about behaviour in general can be drawn. The next stage in the design consists of initial brief exchanges between members of a common interest, i.e. homogeneous, group.

(2) *Common interest groups*

These groups, trios or quartets, consist of managers with similar roles, similar functions, or similar geographical background, who can start to explore their own problems and themes communicating with each other in familiar language. No member of staff is present at this stage, which immediately follows the introductory plenary meeting, unless a group requests clarification. Early on, therefore, participants begin to establish support with others by virtue of their membership of a group consisting of managers with common backgrounds. The content of their task at this stage is to formulate agenda relevant to some common interest that each can take with him to the work group. They meet again at later stages for different purposes.

(3) Work groups

At the core of the design are the heterogeneous groups of nine managers, which have the task of understanding how content and process are interdependent in achieving group objectives. Once there has been an opportunity to share, in a further plenary meeting, the variety of managerial problems which participants have begun to discuss with each other, the first of the work group periods takes place. Here the course members meet in a different setting where they now find themselves members of a group with mixed, perhaps conflicting, interests.

Thus at this stage the course design has already established a replica of institutional life. The members belong to one group where they speak a recognised language; to another group where they must try to understand the language of others whose ideas and backgrounds are unfamiliar; and to a total organisation, represented by a plenary meeting where all participants come together to deal with matters affecting their inter-group requirements.

(4) Consultation groups

For the next 2 days the common interest groups (renamed as consultative groups) and the work groups function alternately. The task of the former has changed and is now concerned with learning about the giving and taking of advice between colleagues. By reason of this alternation, course members experience, in a temporary system, the conflict of interest that flows from simultaneous membership of distinct groups, and learn to sustain the two-way stretch to which they are subjected. Exactly how these different aspects of the week's course develop will be the function of the staff to observe, to describe, and to interpret in relation to the process involved in managing groups. The content or vehicle by means of which such awareness on the part of members is intended to develop is represented by the members' own agendas, brought from their trios and quartets to the work groups.

(5) Theory session: the nature of groups

It is only after sufficient time has elapsed for managers to experience, through their work groups, exactly how each group has been handling its discussions, whether these be contentious or not, that a plenary or intergroup period is included in the course design. This takes the form of a theory presentation by a staff member about 'The Nature of Groups'. The experiences in work groups, however frustrating or uncertain their nature, precede therefore any attempt to draw together more general concepts about groups. The structure is essentially a reflection of the wish to proceed from the known to the unknown; in other words, it supports learning by discovery. Here it is expected (and experience bears out this expectation) that the course participants will relate this talk about groups in general to their own developing perceptions about what is taking place in their work groups.

Thus, about one-third of the way through the course, at the very point where members are feeling that they are lost, that the staff process observations are merely intrusive, unhelpful remarks (not germane to the content discussions), and that confusion is a dominant note, the attempt is made through the plenary discussion to enable participants to see their experiences against a fresh set of concepts. The design is deliberate, giving rise, therefore, to feelings of manipulation, as if the course staff have been keeping these revelations up their sleeve.

(6) *Inter-group exchange*

Not only does the course aim to provide opportunities to look at small groups, it is also concerned — because management involves such experiences — to examine what happens when groups try to work and communicate with each other. About mid-way through the week, therefore, the work groups have the opportunity to share formally their experiences to date, by means of an inter-group exchange, in which two members from each group describe and discuss with each other their separate views of what has occurred in their respective groups. This is arranged as a 'fishbowl' exercise, in which representatives of groups are observed by their course colleagues who have chosen them. Again, not only is content of the formal discussions about work groups important (informal discussions about them will obviously have been held — in the bar, the dining-room, the garden, as in most institutions) but, more relevantly, given the course objectives, the process by which this public exchange takes place acquires significance. Members here have the chance to evaluate the experience of what happens when representatives are faced with conflicting feelings, loyalty to one group (their own work group) yet with a desire to understand the attitudes of people from another group. The criteria for choice of representatives are also reviewed.

(7) *Review and field force analysis*

Underlying the initial attempts to create this type of course was always a belief in the value of 'suspending business' for effecting a review of organisational life and of objectives (in such a way as to appraise groups) as well as individual performance. As in the Leicester University/Tavistock Institute courses, it has been considered essential for managers to have the opportunity in the course itself to look back at what has been happening, to make proposals about what might happen in the future and to come to jointly agreed decisions worked out between the groups about what will best suit the future needs of the course, as a total institution. The participants themselves thus share, with the course staff responsible for the design, in the assessment of the course's relevance. A method for doing this, currently used on these courses, is Field Force Analysis, by use of which managers produce measures of those forces which assist and those which detract from the course objectives. It is hoped that having experienced its usage on the course itself, they will consider using it in the management of organisation elsewhere. The essential feature of this review, with its subsequent decision-making phase element to determine the content of later periods on the course, lies in the occasion which it affords to examine, through staff feedback and guidance, just how the course members, in managing their own temporary institution, proceed with this task. It is possible to draw valuable insights about the dynamics of conflict or of co-operation, with which institutions, through their sub-groups, have to contend. Again, this experiential learning is real, it relates to the activity of the course affecting subsequent activities in the week, and yet it affords a further opportunity to understand the forces, including internal and external influences, such as the competitive pressures and drives, which make up group life. The rational, logical aspects of decision in institutions are seen to be tempered by the irrational, the illogical and the emotional.

In the design the theory period is deliberately placed one-third of the way through the course, thus ensuring that at the mid-way period exchanges between groups, followed by joint reviews take place with pertinent comment from the consultants. The participants will have gained by the time the course is two-thirds through insights about how groups work. The last third of the residential phase, apart from being based on wishes emanating from the review phase, is a preparation for return to the external world. It is at this stage, when awareness of process has been acknowledged, however uncertainly put into words, that the members of each 'work group' can examine their own group's process and expect to find parallels between them and those in groups in which they are members back in their sponsoring organisations. In a sense, the content of the group discussions, towards the latter part of the week's course, becomes concern with the group's own processes and dynamics. The consultant will feel free to engage in discussion with group members about process, even to conduct, where appropriate, brief seminars about organisational theory, aspects of social psychology, the nature of groups. For that reason it will have been necessary for the course staff, at its pre-course meeting, and in the staff meetings, which continue during the residential phase, to have decided what relevant papers on theory should be available if needed. Whatever papers are brought to the course, they are best received only if introduced when members can gain knowledge from them relative to points arising from the course experience itself.

(8) *Final stages*

The final stages of the residential phase attempt to prepare members for return to their organisations, and therefore deal with the relationship between their course experience and the point of entry. It is possible to convey a feeling of wholeness in the shapes of the week's activities by reference back to the topics and questions which members brought to the work groups for discussion. So the trios and quartets, formed originally as groups with a degree of homogeneity, or common interest, are reconstituted and meet immediately prior to the brief plenary session with which this phase of the course concludes. This is to allow members to recall their first uncertain, tentative group meetings, and to attempt to relate the intervening experience of the week to the pressing, urgent tasks they will face beyond the confines of the course. As with a holiday, the descriptions to others not present of an experience not shared by them is likely to prove a frustrating, even fruitless, undertaking. How then can one take up work where it was left? How relate again to colleagues who will be incapable of receiving with comprehension and sympathy one's inability to interpret the significance of the week's events? Thus, the problems of a return to both family and work-place demonstrate in a real and immediate sense the central theme of the course. For an individual to join or re-join groups requires sensitivity about the nature of small groups and the ways in which they function.

However, the ensuing plenary session when participants and staff alike re-convene from their homogeneous groups—for consultants and observers too can benefit from a pause to consider jointly the future against the background of the course—is not an occasion for further public review of groups' process. The need for business now outweighs the need for any suspension of business. On occasions the staff find themselves giving a lead on content, whilst participants, reversing the usual roles, seem to be more concerned with process.

A practical task is provided by a brief discussion of the interim plans for a follow-up meeting, say, after 6 months, with the need to make arrangements, to co-ordinate dates, to consult diaries; in fact, to think immediately of that external world to which everyone now must return. To quote Shakespeare's Edmund in King Lear—'The wheel has come full circle'. Course participants, having shared in a learning experience about the membership and management of small groups, are about to take on more familiar roles again. And so they leave the course, as they joined it, as accountants, industrial engineers, production managers, personnel officers, marketing managers.

(iii) POST-COURSE PHASE

The objectives in providing an occasion for course members to re-convene some 6 months later are:

(1) To evaluate the course's relevance to the roles and functions which people will have taken up again after the residential part of the course.

(2) To re-appraise one's own performance at work and the feelings about one's career development in the light of the course.
(3) To discover the major organisational issues raised since, as a result of attempting to relate 'group dynamics' to problems at work.

Therefore, the members and staff come back to the same conference centre for a period of some $2\frac{1}{2}$ days. The temptation for the staff to concentrate on process comments, to the exclusion of any involvement in the content to be examined, has to be resisted. This brief 'follow-up' activity, in looking back whilst still continuing to look forward, specially to the relevance of group dynamics to problems at work, is one in which staff and members alike share their experiences. Typically, after resuming through the mechanism of work groups, and thereby meeting the need to enjoy a re-union, the course members focus attention on special areas of interest. Case studies of organisational problems can be carried out, frequently by new groupings made up of people who now have a new common interest. Whether individuals wish to discuss with others the self-appraisal already carried out as arranged before coming to the 'follow-up' session is left to them to decide. This is to allow each one to decide how far and in what way he can use the earlier 1 week's experience to seek guidance about his future career, and whether to choose to do so with his own superior at work. Inevitably, the points raised at this post-course meeting relate to questions of organisational complexity back at work. Thus the relevance to this complexity, familiar and perhaps inevitable in any large multi-functional enterprise, of the Practice of Management becomes a topic for consideration. This, in turn, can lead to work between course members, between members and staff, and between members of different and separate courses, in what may generally be described as 'organisation development'.*

4. Staff Roles, What they do and their Relationship to Group Members

Staff roles, like course design are conceived as enabling resources; so that in addition to the importance of *what* a staff member does, there is the importance of the *way* in which he does it.

(i) A staff member takes different roles at different stages and in different situations. To put it briefly, in the early trios and quartets he clarifies—if called upon to do so; in the work group, which is designed to facilitate learning about management as a process, he is an adviser who listens and gives feedback; in his seminar activities on the course he can reinforce learning about, say, leadership and motivation, by drawing on situations experienced by the group; in the small consultative groups he observes and controls.

---

* Organisation Development; we use this term to refer to the activities arising from recognition that a large business organisation is like an organism in that its functioning can be described in terms of a socio-technical system, and that by so doing process and content of its work are seen to be inextricably related.

He must differentiate between these roles clearly, and so emphasise from the start the relationship between clarity of roles and organisational effectiveness. At any stage the consultant must remain consistent with his role, and thus establish his function clearly.

(ii) Returning to what a consultant does, the same distinction between content and process applies. The point of a consultant's intervention in the early stages is often not perceived, as it will refer to the way things are happening in the group rather than to content—and the group does not yet understand process. (As the group develops it finds difficulty in reconciling the consultant's process comments with its own interests in optimising task objectives and balancing this with its own group needs both to avoid fractionating and to cope with other internal forces.)

The consultant does not refuse to answer relevant questions (i.e. those consistent with his role) but if he is asked a question about content (e.g. what is your opinion about the influence of trade unions in industry upon the authority of management) he may indicate why, at that moment, the group wishes him to take over their task rather than carry it out themselves.

One way in which a group may cope with uncertainty is to establish a familiar structure, which often means appointing a chairman and perhaps a secretary. There may be opposition, often unvoiced, to these moves and the consultant notes it, for future reference when opposition becomes overt—usually in some rationalised form. The consultant's intervention is then designed to produce a realisation that a particular structure or procedural form is not a general solution to difficulties of operational functioning. On the other hand, the experience can help later to determine when such a structure or procedure should realistically be brought into play. From the point of view of process, the timing of intervention is crucial, an opportunity for intervening not taken may not recur. Usually, however, the dynamics of the group behaviour are repeated, though in another or disguised form.

In the later stages, the consultant has to exercise self-discipline, through recognising the group's own growth in learning potential, so that he does not intervene in the same way throughout, but allows participants to try their hand on process comment whenever they are ready to do so.

(iii) THE CONSULTANT'S RELATIONSHIP TO THE GROUP

In the early stages a consultant is liable to be the target for hostile feelings, overt or covert, because a group perceives the consultant as having 'failed' to help or lead the group. As time progresses and learning experience grows, group members begin to distinguish between manipulating others, being manipulated and feeling that one is being manipulated. The theme of manipulation itself often becomes a temporary system for learning about integrity, and about recognising when one is either obliged or can choose to conform with certain circumstances. Two forces, but often more, are usually involved; (a) the urge to get on with the job in hand, (b) the effort to provoke the consultant into 'coming clean'.

Later the group is liable to show frustration over failure to achieve goals in content; or the group may want its own survival as its aim, or be reluctant to 'jell' enough because it would become too 'cosy'. In various crises such as these, the group's sense of aggravation may be turned on the consultant for failure to help.

The consultant must understand and learn how best to help the group in these circumstances. He may suspend business to examine those factors that are determining the group's actions. By concentrating on roles, the consultant ensures that he is seen to be concerned only with group development and not with judgements about individual behaviour. Individuals will be learning about, as well as from, each other and may begin to discuss or explore these aspects. The consultant, however, only refers to individuals and their behaviour insofar as it is relevant, and contributes to the group's process task. He must try to avoid becoming defensive.

One specific phenomenon usually occurs about one-third way through the course. It is usually to be associated with the underlying decision-making by the group as to the level of learning with which it will proceed. The group's discovery that the way forward lies in giving self-study and reflection on its own behaviour and ways of working as prominent a place as task achievement, is critical. Once the consultant recognises this movement and decision-making process of the group, he can begin to assume that the group is joining him, and indicating a capacity to share in the other task of looking at process as well as content. Soon afterwards the group often plays its part in recognising the change by sometimes referring to the way in which the consultant has become a 'member'.

(iv) A CONSULTANT HAS TO 'EARN THE RIGHT TO BE TRUSTED'.

To remind himself of incidents in the development of his work group, a consultant may wish to take notes. He may or may not comment on this, but in any case the group is likely to suspect that the notes are for other ulterior purposes, usually because of past association with authority figures displaying judgmental attitudes.

No consultant can expect to be trusted as of right; he has to earn trust. Only through consistency of role and tasks, and certainly not just through techniques used in the course, will the trust and confidence of participants develop. Trust itself will come to be recognised as a process, not a state. Once, however, a 'good enough' shared experience has developed, a slip out of role by the consultant may be forgiven (may even lead to his being seen as human after all), but basic discrepancies can have most damaging effects. All too often, despite an individual's own acute and intuitive observing capacity, a consultant (or a manager) may grossly underestimate that penetrating and subtle sense of the 'music behind the words' which groups use at all times.

5. Findings derived from review of course experience

Firstly it must be acknowledged by anyone who feels it desirable to do this work that a probable outcome will be one's own sense of the wonderful value of such work. One should, therefore, be aware of the easy trap which delusions can provide—that an experience of learning from the 'here and now' will develop for everybody. Although no attempt has yet been made to draw up a typology of causes producing identifiable effects, and especially those which result in difficult experiences for staff and participants alike, nevertheless certain obvious cause-effect relationships do seem clear:

(i) Commitment to the objectives of the course, coupled with a willingness to explore, to try out, by an individual participant, does produce positive attitudes to learning.

(ii) Where an individual feels he has been sent for some vaguely therapeutic purpose, he builds resistance and even rejection against what is to him an intrusive threat.

(iii) Where an individual's own manager is either half-hearted or even highly sceptical, then that individual, whatever he may really feel about the method of learning, will deny the value of the experience.

(iv) Where a staff member displays, however unconsciously, his own uncertainty, or anxiety about himself and his career, or his competence, then this attitude transfers across to course members, who in turn display anxiety and even aggression towards him and the course in general.

(v) Where a sponsoring manager's behaviour belies his words, which may *in appearance only* support such open-ended learning activities as this course, then the subordinate is liable to be guarded in his own behaviour.

(vi) No application of learning from experience is possible in any organisational setting which rewards conformist 'safe' behaviour.

It was in the hope of taking these points into account that membership of the course was controlled by the carefully worded criteria (see section 3) on which the invitations are based.

Naturally it is not always possible to guarantee in advance of each course that members will be paragons of influence, resilience and sensitivity. Indeed, what is essential is that people, with a positive, not negative approach, be encouraged to test themselves out in this temporary system, provided that they receive 'back home' support for their efforts. However, there are sufficient indications now to believe that transference of process awareness to groups in which managers have to work with colleagues is a reality.

6. Evaluation and Organisation Development

In the early courses, participants completed questionnaires on their attitudes and assumptions about management behaviour. Questions based, for example, on concepts about motivation of people, as outlined by writers like McGregor and Herzberg, were answered prior to the course, during the course and at the conclusion. The purpose was to help managers examine any significant behavioural change which might derive from their learning experiences. However, it began to seem that the anxiety of the course staff to prove the relevance of the training was greater than the participants' need to learn. The very process of collecting and comparing the data took on an undue emphasis which interfered with the development of course activity, and hindered the consultants in their principal task. Questionnaires are still occasionally used; for example, as a means of introducing a theory session on motivation, should this be what participants and staff alike feel to be required on any given course. However, no formal evaluation of the courses is conducted in this way, although, currently, an attempt is being made to assess the value of the courses by means of a survey conducted objectively with all previous participants. The participants have, in fact, been used themselves to assist in the final preparation of the questionnaires which a social scientist has suggested.

Because of the obvious difficulty, given the number of variables which can affect both individual and group behaviour in any organisation, no attempt to quantify the value of the courses has been made. Perhaps the most significant outcome is that some course members have taken the idea of suspending business from the temporary system provided by the courses to their places of work.

For instance, individuals have been able to evaluate their careers in the light of their course experience, and groups of managers faced with tasks have suspended business to examine how the work being done (the content) is influenced by the way in which they are doing it (the process).

Action which has stemmed from the recognition of this activity as being of value normally derives from the understanding which develops between a course staff member and a manager, who, through participation in one of the courses, has gained insight about the consultant role in group work. For example, training managers have been able to respond to the wishes of their organisations to adopt a more open appraisal method in order to help create more effective career patterns for managers. The need to do so has arisen from conversations about how relevant the learning is to factories, laboratories, and commercial offices of the Practice of Management. Similarly a number of management teams, including the executive boards of two subsidiary companies, have asked for assistance from training staff in order to carry out the review of their group's effectiveness, in the same way that work groups suspend their business in the courses.

To describe in detail how this awareness of the link between training and operational activity can lead to organisation development would require a separate chapter. Suffice to say, therefore, such transfer of awareness has been found to occur in several of the factories, laboratories and offices.

Some executive managers, in discussion with their training managers, have recognised that there can be value in reviewing, not only structures and roles of managers (i.e. process) but what is still more important, the organisation's concrete objectives and the tasks which flow from them. One factory, where a number of managers have attended the course and whose subordinates have similarly attended 'off-plant' training along these lines, has, through its director's initiative, set up project groups comprising people of different disciplines and functions to examine specific problems. Other parts of the company have not only reviewed the relationship between their objectives and their methods of work, in keeping with the principles of socio-technical systems analysis and development, they have continued to review this content — process interaction, through conferences organised away from their own places of work and, as a result, have effected their own changes.

Now that many seeds have been sown, the future emphasis in the Practice of Management courses will be very much that of training the trainers. The recognition of the role which a staff member can take creatively as consultant to a group has brought new demands. Thus, it is not the intention to overlay the organisation as a whole with courses in behavioural skills, but rather to increase the possibility of learning from work groups, whether these be at board room level or on the shop floor. The trainer, as consultant, has greater opportunities for a more constructive intervention in the work of his managerial colleagues. The development of his competence and skills now becomes a prime requirement, if the various organisations are to gain the optimum benefit from Practice of Management courses.

7. Conclusion

In its evolution the course has changed in emphasis, from a concern with those inter-personal skills required in communicating appraisals to a recognition of the importance of understanding how a group, faced with tasks, carried out those tasks. This, in turn, has enabled managers to appraise not only their own behaviour in relation to work shared with others, but also the corporate nature of such work. Possibilities are opening up for insights gained in training to carry over into new ways of managing groups, in which the values about human behaviour and its link with operational effectiveness can be seen more clearly.

The work place will hopefully be seen increasingly as a socio-technical system, in which, to quote an American author Dr. J. Luft, 'the question of superiority of individual as against group productivity is less important than an understanding of what takes place when people work together'. Perhaps through activities like the Practice of Management with its impact upon a total organisation, we will discover in our contemporary society some of the old values about work and the nature of man, and re-learn how to bring human resources to bear upon human problems.

© 1979 K. B. Low and Harold Bridger

CHAPTER 6

Work in Small Groups: Some Philosophical Considerations

BY B. A. FARRELL

The foregoing chapters have outlined five ways of working with small groups. This work is very extensive, and it relies on various intellectual traditions. What the practitioners have to say is of great interest and, probably, of considerable importance. But just because of all this, the ordinary reader can be forgiven if he comes away suffering from indigestion and some bewilderment at the plate-load of offerings that have been presented to him. It may be worthwhile, therefore, to try to stand back from it all, and to attempt to clarify the character of what has been offered him. This may help to ease the indigestion and dispel the bewilderment.

I

The five contributors have described how small groups have been run, by different organisations, with a view to realising certain aims or ends. Their various procedures reveal some surface similarities and differences. The aim of the work described by Marcus is, at the least, to alter the inmates of the prison in such a manner that, after they are released, they do not find their way back again into the dock in the criminal courts. This is obviously very different from the aim of the work described by the other contributors. Adair is concerned 'to foster the precious resource of leadership', and he tells us about methods used to do this in the Army, and by ACL in industry, commerce and the public service. Coverdale Training aims to train people to get things done when they are working as a team in small groups, in a wide variety of situations, from the managerial boardroom to the shop floor, from government departments to sports clubs. The courses in the practice of management that Low and Bridger describe are to train managers to be more effective, whether at work in the boardroom or cogitating over affairs in the privacy of their own sanctums. In contrast the Grubb Institute — according to Palmer — is concerned 'to improve role-performance' in the work groups of which he is a member, whether he be a business man, a teacher, or a priest.

Furthermore, according to Marcus, Grendon Underwood is designed to work as a therapeutic *institution*, and groups are organised so as to help to produce a 'prison culture', which will serve, it is hoped, to change the prisoner into a person who will not relapse into the arms of the criminal courts. An essential device to help achieve this is the use of the groups to exert pressure on the prison inmates to change certain of their fundamental attitudes so as to bring these into line with the attitudes of society. In contrast with this, none of the other four procedures operates within a residential institution and over long periods of time; and they do not use groups to induce changes in the fundamental attitudes of members. But they do use groups to change people by giving them skills they did not possess before and, according to Marcus, Grendon also uses groups for this purpose with prison officers. It is clear that the methods they all use for this purpose differ quite considerably *inter se*.

Now let me ignore the contribution from Marcus for the present. It seems clear that Adair and the others do describe their methods in ways which—if adequate—reveal that these methods have one important complex and obscure feature in common. Thus, Adair tells us (p. 6) that 'ACL training does include the transmission of some knowledge. It is based on the assumption that each of the main research approaches towards the understanding of leadership contains some truth which course participants will find both interesting and relevant to their responsibilities. In ACL these approaches are summed up in Adair's 'trefoil model' (p. 9). He claims in this way to 'reach an understanding of leadership which is sufficiently specific and concrete to allow us to base training upon it' (p. 10). He concludes by referring to 'the small plenary group system' he has described, and claims that 'there can be no doubt about . . . its effectiveness for adults seeking to understand and practise leadership . . .' (p. 17). Waterston speaks in a similar vein. 'There is a range of themes', he tells us, 'which underlies all forms of Coverdale training' (p. 19). 'The learning method used on Coverdale courses is designed to encourage insight and develop understanding and skill in bringing about improvement' in the human areas on which the themes have a bearing (pp. 19, 20). In the learning that course members go through, they appear to make discoveries about the ways in which they can operate effectively in various sorts of teams. These discoveries appear to be necessary (though obviously not sufficient) conditions for the insight into, and understanding of, what is happening in their teamwork—which Coverdale training aims to help them acquire. Low and Bridger offer 'a theoretical and conceptual framework' (pp. 85 ff.). In order for course members 'to gain . . . a fresh insight into management' (p. 90), it is necessary for them to catch on to and to acquire some skill in actually applying the concepts and generalisations embodied in the theoretical and conceptual framework that is offered to members (see, e.g., p. 93). By so doing—by going through these courses—it is hoped to give members 'insight' and 'sensitivity'—which they did not have before—into the life and working of groups and their members. Palmer speaks in a very similar way. He sets out the 'theoretical assumptions' used by the Grubb Institute, and they contain a large battery of concepts and generalisations. He 'indicates the bearing of some (of the) key concepts' in the efforts of group members to learn from the courses and 'to extend their own understanding of group processes and of authority and leadership' (pp. 44, 45, 57).

Well, what is the important common feature that the methods possess according to this description of them?

Observe that Adair *et al.* do all use words and expressions such as the following: 'understanding', 'insight(s)', 'knowledge', 'sensitivity', 'awareness'. It seems clear that they use these words to help them to say three things.

(1) That they, Adair *et al.*, do understand, or have an understanding of, what happens in their groups; they have insight(s) into the sorts of things that happen; they know what goes on in them; and so forth. In contrast, the average new member of a group does not possess this understanding, etc.

(2) That they, Adair *et al.*, run their groups in ways which will help the members to acquire this insight, develop this understanding of, or knowledge about, what happens in groups.

(3) That this gain in insight, or understanding, or sensitivity, or knowledge, or awareness, is a *necessary* condition for members to acquire the relevant skills they are trying to give the group members.

On the description which Adair *et al.* give us of their group methods, all the methods outlined make these three claims. This is the important feature which the methods have in common on the description of them which we are considering.

II

How adequate is this description? How adequate, therefore, is this whole way of presenting and thinking about what Adair *et al.* are doing? It is very natural, of course, for them to describe their work in this way. For these group methods have taken their rise (in particular) from work in social psychology, individual psychology, and psychoanalysis; and workers in these fields are also concerned to arrive at understanding, knowledge, insight, and so on. It is also very tempting for Adair *et al.* to describe their work in the way that they do, because on this description it embodies very large claims; and it is tempting to speak like this about the work just because this is a large or inflated way of talking, which may help each organisation to sell its own wares in the market. As Adair has said very shrewdly in discussing the limitations of ACL, 'When commercial considerations crowd in even a modicum of disinterestedness is difficult to maintain' (p. 15).

Unfortunately, in my judgement, this way of describing what Adair *et al.* are doing is very difficult to defend. For it is far too simple-minded.

To say that John Jones understands the tides is to say that he has at his disposal a body of concepts and generalisations which represent the truth about tidal phenomena, and that he is able to exercise, or apply, these concepts and generalisations to order and explain any instance of, or segment of, tidal behaviour. To say that an operator X — using one of the four group methods we are considering — understands, or has an understanding of, his groups, or what happens in his groups—to say this is to say that operator X has at his disposal a body of concepts and generalisations which represent the truth about his groups, and which he is able to exercise, or apply, to order and explain any instance or segment of his own group phenomena. Well, where are these bodies of truth that our operators, Adair *et al.* each possess? Can we say that the trefoil model (of Adair), the theoretical framework (of Palmer), and so on, each constitute a body of truth we are looking for?

It is very doubtful whether we can say that the sets of concepts and generalisations Adair *et al.* each use constitute the body of truth we require. For the concepts they each employ are (typically) very vague, and it is doubtful whether reasons can be found which are good enough to oblige us to use *any* set of them. This is evident when we look at the empirical generalisations in which these concepts function. The generalisations are (typically) so vague that it is uncertain what is required to establish or to refute them. Consider, for example, Coverdale's generalisation that 'the building up of confidence, in the light of successful experience . . . is essential to the learning aims of management training' (p. 22). Or take Low and Bridger's number (i): 'That while a group consists of individuals, the group itself exists as an entity with an identifiable culture' of its own (p. 85). What would we have to do to confirm or to refute either of these generalisations? It is very far from clear. So the body or bodies of truth that Adair *et al.* require—on the description of their methods we are considering—do not appear to exist.

It is obvious what the general reason is that plunges Adair *et al.* into these difficulties. The description we are considering commits them logically to making claims about their groups which are true. If we describe, for example, Palmer's work by saying that he understood what happened in a particular group at a certain time, we are saying that statement p (which expresses what he understood) is a true statement. Obviously—because it is absurd to say: 'He understood, etc., but p is false'.

Therefore we cannot say *simpliciter* that what Adair *et al.* have an understanding of, or an insight into, etc., is how groups work, or what happens in them, and so forth. Likewise, we cannot say *simpliciter* that what course members acquire is an understanding of, or insight into, etc., how groups work, and so forth. Of course it is very natural and tempting to adopt this simple-minded way of talking—because it seems so commonsensical and because there is no obvious and acceptable alternative available. But this simple-minded way of talking just will not do. It may be some comfort to Adair *et al.* to point out that they are not alone in being confronted by the problem of how to describe what they are doing; the whole world of psycho-therapy is confronted by the same problem, and psycho-therapists are also floundering in the ramified complexities that it generates.

III

How, then, *should* we describe and speak about what Adair *et al.* are doing? If the large or strong or inflated description which Adair *et al.* themselves offer, and which we have just examined, is too simple-minded, how should this description be qualified and amended? I doubt whether this question can be answered at the present time in a way that will be generally acceptable. For these questions raise problems that have not yet been solved. And, when group operators are confronted by the difficulties we have just outlined, they are apt to be thrown into confusion and even anger; they start fudging and offering all manner of vague and, manifestly, unsatisfactory qualifications to their simple-minded description.

I shall now try to grasp the nettle here and offer an alternative description of what Adair *et al.* are doing. I offer it as a means of clarifying the problem, and of exposing the logical difficulties with which group operators seem to be faced.

Let us look again at what Adair *et al.* are each doing. As we have seen, they each organise their groups somewhat differently in order to try to realise their various aims. Naturally, therefore, these groups produce different sorts of material—which has to be put into order. Now each operator proceeds to do this—to put his material into order—by picking out a pattern of features that he judges his material exhibits. He embodies the upshot of this ordering in a set of concepts and generalisations. These jointly constitute what can be called his Way of Talking, or WOT for short; and he uses it to train the new group member, Smith, to spot the pattern of features that his WOT picks out. Thus, for example, Adair uses his trefoil scheme to help members 'to notice' when, for instance, they are overlooking the needs of the individual member; Low and Bridger use their theoretical framework to help group members 'to notice' the influence of the 'hidden agenda' in the group. When Smith gives the operator evidence that he (Smith) can use his WOT, in some measure, and that Smith is using this WOT to control his own behaviour in relevant situations, then the operator will say that Smith has now acquired some insight and understanding—that he now knows more about what was going on—that he has some grasp of, or sensitivity to, what happens, and is ready perhaps for an advanced course. And so on.

When Smith has acquired these skills, it is natural for the operator to talk about Smith by saying that he has now acquired some insight and understanding. He can speak like this without being misleading for *all* he is claiming here—on the description I am offering—is that Smith has insight and understanding, awareness and sensitivity, etc., *in the sense that* he can pick out, or notice, the features of the group material which the operator's WOT point to, he can control his own behaviour in the light of these features, and so forth. And this, of course, is a weak, or watery, sense of the expression 'insight and understanding', etc. What the operator is *not* claiming, expressly or by implication, on this description is that Smith has insight and understanding, etc., in the strong sense, according to which he now has the ability to produce statements about the workings of groups which are true *simpliciter*. All the operator is claiming for Smith, and all he seems entitled to claim, is insight and understanding in the weaker or watery sense; and not in the second and much stronger sense we have distinguished—the sense which is involved in the large and inflated description we have already considered. These two senses are liable to be confused; and it is very advisable that we should not confuse them. If operators are trapped into supposing that Smith has acquired insight and understanding in the strong sense, then they will be tempted to make large and unjustified claims on their own behalf. On the other hand, if operators claim merely that all they achieve for group members is insight and understanding in the weak sense, then their claim is a modest one and seems to be well supported. What is more, this modest stand will also help to stop them selling themselves in the market by misleading exaggeration and inflation.

This, then, is an alternative description of what Adair *et al.* are doing—one designed to remove the central difficulty produced by their own large or strong description of their methods. What is more, this alternative description has an additional merit. It helps to bring out that, even if Adair *et al.* are only making the modest claim outlined, this claim is surrounded by still further limitations.

It is clear that the insight, etc., which one operator provides for his group members is dependent upon the particular perspective he adopts on small groups and their functioning. Coverdale training gives one angle of view, Low and Bridger quite another. Indeed, it is all too clear that the four operators we are considering all adopt perspectives that differ from one another to a greater or lesser degree. Furthermore, when an operator uses his WOT in the way described above, there is some empirical evidence to suggest that he helps *to produce* group material that will fit in with his own WOT. (Such evidence is to be found in work on psychotherapy and related studies.) If this is true of the groups we are dealing with, then it follows that the use of a WOT is a self-confirmatory procedure. An operator gets back from his group's material that—in general—supports his own view of what is going on and how to proceed. His method helps to manufacture material which will support the method. Therefore, the insight and understanding, etc., that the operator helps his groups to acquire are not only dependent on his own perspective; they are also dependent on the very method he uses. This conclusion has an important implication. It means that if an operator wishes to claim that this insight and understanding, etc., give members access to the truth about groups, and the like, then they cannot give him a truth that is independent of the perspective and the method used by the operator. Their 'truth' is relative to, and so dependent on, the perspective and method employed. Therefore, they cannot be regarded as objectively true or adequate, and the like. The implications of this conclusion are large and cannot be pursued here. Suffice to say that it imposes on the operators an additional reason for modesty and caution, and it debars them from claiming that they have insight or understanding, etc.—just like that—into what happens in the groups they run.[1]

IV

From all this, it is evident that we cannot show—and no one can argue—that any *one* of the group methods outlined in the previous chapters is nearer to the truth about what happens in groups than any of the others. We cannot show that any one method has a better grasp of group working than any other. As far as truth claims are concerned, there is little or nothing to choose between them. Therefore we cannot show that any one method is superior to another, or to the rest, on this ground.

Nevertheless, it might be argued that—in spite of all the difficulties raised so far—we *can* show one WOT, and connected mode of operation, to be better than the others *if* we can show that this WOT, and its mode of operation, produces *better results* than the others. If we could succeed in showing this, then we would have some grounds, and perhaps good grounds, for saying that this WOT, and its mode of operation, had a better grasp than the others of, for example, management problems, of what happens in board rooms, and so on. There is a comparable argument about psychoanalytic schools. If we could show that, for example, Jungian analysts had significantly better therapeutic results than the analysts of other schools, then we would have some grounds, and perhaps good grounds, for saying that Jungians have a better grasp of mental functioning and malfunctioning than other schools of analysts.

Unfortunately this argument runs into serious objections. It presupposes that there is a straightforward matter-of-fact, or empirical, connection between the use of a particular WOT and the good results that (we are supposing) it and its connected mode of operation produce. But it is very doubtful whether the connection is an empirical one with all, or even any, of the four modes of operation we are considering. Look at Palmer's mode of operation, for example. Consider the state of affairs that he hopes to bring about (namely, role improvement of members), and the Bion-like WOT Palmer uses in his efforts to achieve this end. Now consider the statement: It is quite possible for group members to improve their roles markedly *without* appreciating the features of group situations that his Bion-like WOT helps them to notice. Let us call this statement 'q'. Can Palmer assert q or not? If he *can*, then the connection between a Bion-like WOT and role improvement is an empirical one. It just happens, as a matter of fact, to be the case that the use of a Bion-like WOT helps them to improve their roles. But if he cannot say q in his discourse—if he cannot say that it is possible for members to improve roles without appreciating a Bion-like WOT—then the connection for him is a logical one. Now his actual remarks suggest that he cannot say q in his own discourse; for he seems to have built into the concept of his aim (role improvement) the appreciation of a Bion-like WOT. On the other hand, if Palmer does not want to claim that the connection between the WOT and his aim is either an empirical or a logical one, then what *does* he want to claim? What *is* the connection between them? It remains quite unclear.

If this objection is sound, and if it also applies to the other modes of operation as well, then this objection strongly suggests that the aims of the operators, and the differences between these aims, need further preliminary study. This is obvious. For if Palmer uses 'better manager' (or 'better teacher', etc.) in such a way that it is logically true to assert that 'a better manager is one who has come to appreciate his (Palmer's) Bion-like WOT', and if (say) Coverdale does *not* use 'better manager' in this way, then the differences in aims of our various operators are liable to become important, confusing and self-obstructive.

We can appreciate this by considering some analogous examples. The medical profession seems to be quite unclear about the general overall end or aim of its activity—namely, health or good health or better health, or whatever words and expressions we use to name this end. But this does not matter in the ordinary run of cases in ordinary medicine. For doctors are not, in general, split into various groups, with different aims, such that one group has an aim defined in part in terms of taking regular doses of aspirin, whereas another group has another aim defined in part in terms of eating vegetables grown only from compost. If this were the situation in ordinary medicine, then the medical world would be even more conceptually confusing a place than it is already, and obviously such differences would serve to obstruct the practice of medicine itself.

Of course, this is a fanciful example. But when we consider the position of contemporary psychiatry, we are faced by a situation that is not fanciful at all, and that is close to the situation of our own group operators. It is orthodox to say that the end or aim of psychiatric work is the achievement of mental health; and it is very evident that psychiatrists are also unclear about the nature of this aim. But in psychiatry this unclarity *may* be serious—in contrast with ordinary medicine—because psychiatrists *do* seem to be split into various groups with somewhat different aims, and these differences are not always made explicit. Thus, for example, psychiatrists who practise behaviour therapy seem to pursue an aim (namely, perhaps, symptom removal) that is different from psychiatrists in the psychoanalytic tradition, whose aim is (perhaps) personal reconstruction and greater self-awareness. It also seems clear that these different aims are defined, or explicated, in part in terms of the methods the practitioners advocate and practise—behaviour therapy and psychoanalysis. We all know that psychiatrists are on the defensive at the present time. I suspect that this is due in part to the fact that they are confused about their aims. I suspect, also, that part of the public scepticism about psychiatry takes its rise from the public's sense that psychiatrists are advocating various methods for different aims; and that these differences tend to be covered up under a blanket term such as 'mental health'.

If all this is so, then obviously these differences in aims between psychiatrists are important, confusing and a hindrance to their work. But it is worth observing that such differences in aims, in the 1920s and 1930s, between psychoanalytic and orthodox psychiatry, did not stop analysts and psychotherapists from selling themselves in a big way to the public in the United States of America at that time. If, however, psychiatrists in this country today were to advertise and produce propaganda for their own procedures (chemotherapy or individual psychoanalysis or behaviour therapy, or whatever), then I believe that they would only be able to do so with a very bad conscience. Happily, they are not legally permitted to advertise, etc., and hence they are not tempted to ignore the restraints of conscience.

Now let us return to our group operators. If the analogy with ordinary and psychiatric medicine is worth taking seriously, then it seems very reasonable to demand of group operators that they should be careful and cautious. They should try strenuously to clarify their aims — to tell us what, to each of them, constitutes a 'better manager' (or 'better teacher', etc.); and to make clear how their methods are logically related to their aims. When they do each advertise and advocate their own brand of method and aims, they should do so with caution and humility. For they must avoid the charge that they are trying 'to con' industry, the civil service and others, into spending thousands of pounds annually on methods of unproven worth in pursuit of aims that are obscure.

But let us suppose that the methods are *not* unproven. And let us suppose further that we can show quite conclusively that one WOT and its operators produce 'better results' than their competitors on some generally accepted criterion of 'better results'. Of course, this does little or nothing, in itself, to show that these operators really have a better grasp of how groups work, or management functions and so forth than their competitors. For these superior results may be the outcome of *other* things. It is a well-known fact that groups are powerful agents of personal transformation; and it is arguable that the sources of their power lie in the group situation itself, not in the particular WOT used to operate it.[2] If this is so, then the (alleged) fact that Adair *et al.* are one and all successful in getting good results gives us (in itself) little ground for saying that any of them has a good grasp of what is going on in their own groups, in board rooms, on the shop floor, and in similar places.

However, if we suppose that the use of one method produces demonstrably better results than its competitors, then we would probably not worry very much in practice about the reasons for its pragmatic superiority. We would not be worried as to whether this method really does give us a good grasp of what goes on in its own groups, in board rooms, etc. The fact that we could not explain its success would probably not upset us any more than, for example, the fact that certain drugs are apparently effective in alleviating and controlling depression, and yet we cannot explain why this is the case.

V

But what results *do* the four methods achieve? It seems evident that both Low and Bridger and Palmer are not interested in follow-up studies and results. What they do offer by way of evaluation is far too weak even to constitute reasonable support, let alone proof, of anything. At most what they offer can be said *to suggest* that some good comes out of what they do. Adair is interested in getting at results, and what he offers by way of follow-up is stronger than what Low and Bridger and Palmer present. In contrast, Waterston makes it clear that Coverdale Training is not only interested in follow-up work, but actively initiates and co-operates in the running of evaluation studies. These give us some ground for saying that Coverdale Training does achieve results.

Of course, what we lack in respect of all four contributions are follow-up studies presenting comparative material from control groups, which have not been trained by Adair *et al.* but which have been trained in some other way, or not been trained at all. It is necessary to have material from adequately designed control studies, in order to establish that these four modes of training achieve anything. Since this material does not exist, we have to conclude that it has not yet been established that these four modes of training do achieve anything.

There is an immediate consequence from all this. No one organisation out of our four is in a logical position to use the (alleged) results of its training to support the contention that it has a grasp of what happens in groups, which is superior to that of its competitors. No doubt, it is plausible to say that each organisation has *some* grasp of what happens in groups in the sense of 'grasp' involved in the weaker description of what Adair *et al.* are doing (see above, pp. 106–8); and that each has a rather *different* grasp from the others, because they each organise their groups in different ways. But no one organisation can claim—on grounds of better results—to have a better or greater understanding or knowledge of what happens in groups than the others.

VI

Suppose, then, that a firm or a manager or an individual school teacher (say) is confronted by these four modes of training. Which should the firm or person choose?

From what has been said so far, there is insufficient reason to make him choose any. It would be quite rational of him to say: 'Thank you very much, but I am having none of you.' If, however, he does decide to choose, which one should he take? Quite obviously, a rational choice here will depend (in part) on the particular situation of the individual firm, or the particular job or make up of the individual person concerned. Thus, it would be more sensible (perhaps) for a school teacher to join a Palmer group than a Coverdale one; and for a large organisation to put its staff through ACL or Coverdale Training rather than the small group work of Palmer and of Low and Bridger. But are there any *general* reasons—independent of particular situations and circumstances—good enough to make us choose one mode of training rather than another? Suppose it had been discovered that, irrespective of relevant individual differences and differences between group situations, it was universally or usually the case that Bion's basic assumptions are at work in an influential and generally obstructive way. We might then possess a good and quite general reason for choosing Palmer's mode of training—at least as a first stage. But no discoveries of this sort appear to have been made. So the answer to our question seems to be: No, there are no general reasons available which are good enough to make us choose one mode of training rather than another.

VII

Now let us return to the narrative by Marcus on the work at Grendon Underwood.

This escapes most of the doubts that have been raised about the other four contributions. In one place, it is true, Marcus does speak of making 'the group more aware of what is happening within itself'; and he defines this awareness in terms of 'greater sensitivity'. He speaks here in the simple-minded, unqualified, way which I have criticised. The fact that he speaks like this may be a manifestation of his own failure to draw explicitly for himself the distinction between the strong (or inflated) and the weaker (or modest) descriptions which can be given of his own work at Grendon. But, in general, Marcus does not make truth claims which are difficult to sustain about the groups in the prison. This is a helpful stance. For in doing therapeutic work with groups, there is no need—in spite of the widespread, standard practice to the contrary—for a group operator to commit himself to claim that his interpretations are true. All he need say is that he had a hunch, or some reason, for suspecting that this or that interpretation, presented at a certain time, would help the group members a little along the road of change for the better. Obviously, a group operator (like Marcus) uses a very technical WOT in his work; but all he need do with it is to use it instrumentally to generate interpretations, and other moves. There is no logical or practical need for him to claim any truth value for his WOT. And, happily, Marcus does not seem to do so. Moreover, he takes as an end, or aim, of the training at Grendon the non-reappearance of the prisoner in the dock. This end is logically independent of the means used to achieve it, and therefore of the WOT used at Grendon; and it is an objective aim, in that it is independent of personal assessments by prisoners, or operators, or anyone else. Furthermore, there is some evidence that the method used produces some beneficial results.

Marcus is also to be commended for the great modesty and sceptical realism with which he presents the work at Grendon. At the same time he also mentions obliquely an argument of quite a different sort from those usually canvassed to justify an institution such as Grendon. Grendon is justified, he suggests, because—irrespective of follow-up results—it attempts 'to create a more humane and civilised prison'; and this is an intrinsically desirable state of affairs. In mentioning this argument, Marcus raises reflections of general interest and importance.

It could be argued that it is intrinsically desirable that all of us—whether company managers, or shop floor stewards or teachers—should carry out our daily work in a way we would ordinarily and naturally describe as one which showed discrimination in inter-personal matters, which showed the necessary sensitivity to the feelings and attitudes and difficulties of others, and so on. This is desirable in itself in the same way as it is desirable that people in general should be educated to realise their potentialities. If a person is capable of, and interested in, being educated in History or Philosophy, then it is a good thing for him to be educated in this way. But it is obviously inappropriate, the argument continues, to demand an evaluation and follow-up study of all those who have had an education in History or in Philosophy. Likewise, it is inappropriate to demand the same thing of those managers, and others, who have received courses of training in leadership, the practice of management and the like. No doubt, these people *will* be better managers and teachers, and so on, as a result of their course training. But the extra dividends they bring in will be indirect and subtle, and not open to adequate quantitative assessment by our present crude methods of scientific investigation.

There would be nothing absurd or unreasonable in Adair *et al.* defending their work in this way—in the same way, that is, in which we defend a higher general education for those who can benefit from it. But if Adair *et al.* were to take this road, they could only defend their work *adequately* if they regarded and treated it as part of an educational enterprise. This is a very large requirement. For one thing, education is a slow business, and participants would probably have to attend for much longer periods than Adair *et al.* employ in their courses. (We may have to envisage periods of in-service training.) More important still, for this defence to carry conviction, Adair *et al.* would have to show that their courses could form part of an intellectual and practical discipline taught at University level; and hence that they could stand up to examination in a context where fundamental criticism and enquiry are taken for granted and actively pursued.

This context is imperative. For in its absence the operators (and their colleagues) may tend to degenerate into hacks, each applying his own pet procedures in isolation from the thought and practice of other workers. When an operator becomes isolated, he is apt to be weighed down by personal uncertainties about his work—uncertainties that render him incapable of, and indeed uninterested in, communicating with others outside of his own organisation. But to live and work like this—in fear of rational evaluation—is to tread the road to decay.

So if the courses of training offered by Adair *et al.* and others, can be made acceptable to Universities and Polytechnics, then the contributions they each have to offer will stand a good chance of being clarified and fostered. Perhaps this volume will do something to encourage developments in this direction.

References

1. In the *Tractatus Logico-Philosophicus*, at 6.341, Wittgenstein asks us to imagine a white surface with irregular black spots, and how we can bring 'the description of the surface to a unified form' by covering the surface with a sufficiently fine network of squares, and

how we can also do this with a network of a triangular or hexagonal mesh.
This example repays study, and will help to bring out some of the difficulties in the alternative description I have offered of how to bring group material to a unified form.
For the problem as it arises in the world of psychotherapy, see Farrell, B. A. (1972) 'The Validity of Psychotherapy', *Inquiry*, 15, 146–70.

2. See, for example: Robert R. Blake and Jane S. Mouton, 'The experimental investigation of interpersonal influence', Ch.6 in *The Manipulation of Human Behaviour*, Albert D. Biderman and Herbert Zimmer (Eds.) 1961. Wiley; and Richard L. Bednar and G. Frank Lawlis, 'Empirical Research in Group Psychotherapy', Ch.21 in *Handbook of Psychotherapy and Behaviour Change*, Allen E. Bergin and Sol L. Garfield (Eds.) 1971. Wiley.

© 1979 B. A. Farrell

CHAPTER 7

Some Psychological and Practical Considerations

BY B. BABINGTON SMITH

Section 1

After reading the five contributions from Adair to Palmer the reader may think that, in spite of the connections indicated in the introduction, the differences in the descriptions preclude any useful comparison or generalisation about work in small groups. The situations described have, however, a number of features in common, and it is important to notice what some of them are.

It is, for instance, characteristic of small group situations that members of the group are together for periods of time. This leads to interaction between members and calls to mind Homan's[1] hypotheses 'that persons who interact frequently with one another tend to like one another' and 'the more frequently persons interact with one another the more alike in some respects their activities and sentiments tend to become'.

Again it is characteristic of small groups that acquaintanceship develops; people get to know each other better. By 'getting to know' I mean learning such things as what others can do, how they think, what they like or dislike, or what their aims are. There is growth of mutual confidence, in the sense that each learns how far others in the group can be relied on, and what they are capable of. There is growth of common experience. This can lead, as is illustrated by Low and emphasised by Waterston, to a basis for communication and thence, as is explicit in the Coverdale method, to a common language and a common framework of ideas.

Enthusiasm is often generated and may be turned to account; but its existence in a group does not, *per se*, entail the activities of the group being useful or desirable.

In addition, in the training situations considered, participants have, initially at least, the expectation of progress; they have the help of someone who has experience of whichever method is being used; the staff have enthusiasm, competence and sincerity; participants are detached, in their groups, from other affairs and have freedom to explore and to experiment with unfamiliar methods where there is low risk and promise of confidentiality, except in the situation described by Marcus, where confidentiality was deliberately broken down for adequate reasons set out in his chapter.

Thus there are extensive and deep seated similarities between the methods, which all point to processes that strengthen relationships within a group. The evidence may therefore be interpreted to indicate that a number of the ways in which a small group becomes powerful are not specific to a particular method but characterise them all.

The situation also has features in common with the Hawthorne experiment, in that small groups are isolated and given some autonomy, and concentrated attention by staff; if their *esprit de corps* develops, its value is not to be depreciated by saying that some of what happens can be explained as a Hawthorne effect.

Section 2

The claim for any method that it is unique can be defended by showing that it has features not shared with other methods. The study of these features may show what a particular method is useful for, or for whom; but such uniqueness does not warrant a claim that this or that method is the only useful one, to the exclusion of other methods. Incidentally, that a particular method has special qualities which make it useful to some people may mean, at the same time, that others, perhaps just as able and competent, find it has little to offer to them.

I now consider a number of important features of small group methods and try to show how they relate to the five methods described.

(a) THE NATURE OF SMALL GROUPS

By some operators, the group is considered as an entity, by others as a collection of individuals. For instance, Low's first theoretical assumption is that while 'a group consists of individuals it is itself an entity with a culture of its own. The group develops a life of its own, it has the capacity to change and to learn'. The question of the status of group decisions is a matter of concern to some participants. Whether for instance a decision by one member can be binding on a group, or whether open assent by all is necessary or to what extent a view held by a majority should prevail, and what is the position about collective responsibility.

When, on the other hand, the group is regarded as a collection of individuals, the relationships between individuals are studied and such matters as individual aims become highly relevant.

Both Low and Palmer emphasise the importance of what is happening 'here and now' in the group. Adair and Waterston are concerned with individuals as well as groups, while Marcus seems to be interested primarily in the development of individuals.

Overlapping both concepts of a group is the concept of a team, if defined as a group in which the individuals have a common aim and in which the jobs and skills of each member fit in with those of the others, as—to take a very mechanical and static analogy—in a jigsaw puzzle pieces fit together without distortion and together produce some overall pattern. Teamwork is given prominence by Waterston and Adair; I must admit that I remain in doubt whether Low or Palmer would use the word Team in the sense just given.

(b) THE SIZE OF SMALL GROUPS

The term 'small groups', in the present context, is used to cover groups of any number up to 24 or so. This range can be sub-divided, into 4 or fewer, 5 to 8, 9 to 15, and more than 15.

The bulk of the work is in groups either of 5 to 8 (Waterston and Adair) or 9 to 15 (Palmer, Low and sometimes Adair). Marcus does not state what sizes are used, but I understand they are usually in the range 6 to 10.

For training, the advantages of 5 to 8 are that members of the group become acquainted relatively quickly; that it is not easy for members to 'opt out' and remain silent, that it is relatively easy to obtain opinions or information from all present, and that the amount of information so obtained can be collated and assimilated. It is also relatively easy for each to find some way of contributing to the proceedings of the group. But it is clear that the staff-participant ratio has to be high.

With 9 to 15, those who use this range see as advantages that only some need take active part in what is going on, that members may sit back, observe proceedings and remain unnoticed. More members may need to become observers, since practical considerations limit the choice of activities in which such numbers can contribute. It becomes appreciably more time consuming for all to contribute views and opinions, and more onerous to comprehend the meaning and implications of them if they are obtained.

Small groups of 4 or fewer can be useful for specific purposes, e.g. for meetings of representatives of larger groups (Low, Waterston), while the larger groups, round the 20 mark, are useful for plenary sessions and where organisational structure is under examination.

It is important to remember that nothing learnt about the merits of this or that size of group for purposes of training points directly to the merits of those sizes of group in *other* situations.

(c) THE COMPOSITION OF GROUPS

Is regarded by most practitioners as of great importance. The governing principle is that a fair degree of heterogeneity is desirable. The variables considered in reaching a heterogeneous mix may vary from one situation to another. For instance, the variables considered in a situation where all participants come from different organisations (e.g. some courses by Palmer, Waterston, Adair) may not be the same as those when all are drawn from within a single organisation (e.g. Marcus or Low). (One of the dullest groups I myself can remember was one composed of 7 training officers.) Any rules about the composition of groups are based on experience in training situations.

(d) PROCESS AND CONTENT OF ACTIVITIES

In any activity one may distinguish between what is done and how it is done; for instance, 'Goodbye' may be said with deep regret or great relief. This distinction has been given great prominence in small group work. It is customary, with some variation of usage, to speak of the 'how' as 'process' while the 'what' is referred to as the 'content', the 'task', or even the 'content of the task'.

Among the five authors, Palmer and Marcus appear to discuss process most. Palmer makes little mention of content or task; Marcus tells us something of the content of the task tackled in the training groups for group-leaders, but very little of the content of the tasks for groups of inmates, beyond saying that the inmates are encouraged to bring their problems to their group.

Low stresses the point that the process in a task is related to the content. Perhaps his clearest illustration of this comes in his Section 4(i) where he describes how the role of the consultant changes from one stage to another in the Practice of Management course.

Coverdale and Adair give prominence to tasks, though both are also concerned with human interaction. In Adair's system the relationship between content and process in a task is indicated by the overlap, in his trefoil diagram, of the needs of the task with the needs of the group and the needs of the individual, but he does little to suggest how participants are to make use of his schematic device. How for instance is one helped to cope with an individual by seeing that he is tactless, or with a group by seeing that it has a scapegoat or has low morale, if one does not already know how to do so?

An answer could be that taking Adair's advice, and hence thinking not in terms of failings but of needs, leads one not to negative measures of constraint or palliation but rather to positive measures of support and help.

Waterston in his account does not refer explicitly to process, but it is his use of words that conceals a strong preoccupation with it. Both in his section on observation and on planning co-operation, to take examples, it is obvious that process is being studied and that participants obtain practice in dealing with matters of process.

Direct comparisons are very difficult here because it is clear that the terms 'process' and 'task' have somewhat different meanings in the five methods. I have tried to employ the terms in their common usage.

It is very usual in everyday life for people to concentrate on what they are doing and to neglect or be unaware of how they do it, and this is especially so of how they interact with other people. In training the emphasis on process is an example of the use of a legitimate educational device to draw attention to features normally overlooked or neglected. It could be objected, however, as a matter of observation, that the concentration of emphasis on process as such can produce an unbalanced approach subsequently in the world of affairs.

Unless interest in process is balanced by a concern for standards of performance, cosy groups result, pleasant to belong to, but unable or little inclined to do useful work.

(e) HIDDEN AGENDA

Low's sixth theoretical assumption is 'that, as in psychoanalysis, what remains unexpressed, even hidden, can be vital to the elucidation of why certain actions take place'.

Several situations can be distinguished under the heading 'what remains unexpressed'.

(i) As Low suggests, a member of the group may have 'hidden agenda'; he may for instance have aims that are deliberately concealed. Such a situation may be resolved when the 'hider' comes to realise that his hidden aims are compatible with those of the group.

Waterston considers how to resolve a variant of this case, where members of a group are unintentionally working to different aims. The trend in the Coverdale method is to forestall such situations by encouraging co-operation and frankness.

(ii) There may be information that a member does not reveal because of its probable effect on others. Here, resolution may come about if he sees that his fear of being shamed by disclosure, or of seeming rude or boastful, is groundless in a setting where revealing what he had withheld is seen to be appropriate frankness or a revelation of useful resources.

(iii) When information or an inference is not supplied by a member because he is not aware of its relevance, or even of its existence. In such a case, restructuring of available information may allow him to see some principle he had not previously seen, or to grasp the relevance of something he already knew.

Thus in all three cases what had been unexpressed may be revealed by the member concerned either as a result of a process of learning or of 'restructuring' accompanied by insight.

For those who operate with psychoanalytical concepts, among them Low, Palmer and probably Marcus, there is a fourth possibility.

(iv) That material has been repressed. *Ex hypothesi*, this material is not available, though it is held possible to recover it by the application of techniques and concepts based on psychoanalytic theory. These are available to the group's consultant.

In contrast to the first three cases, the fourth requires that someone with theoretical knowledge (the consultant) offers the group an interpretation which they may accept, or not. Thus the consultant operates from a position of advantage (having knowledge of the theory) and has power since he can offer interpretation not available to the uninitiated. Insofar as the group accept the interpretation they are drawn to accept the theory too. Piquancy is added to the situation when some participants find the interpretation ridiculous or distasteful.

(f) THEORY AND EXPERIENCE

The methods differ as to whether they stem from and rely on theory, as do Palmer, Low and Marcus, or like Waterston and to some extent Adair, rely primarily on experience and on what individuals and groups discover for themselves. Where there is reliance on theory, recourse to it may offer 'explanations' for situations that have arisen and some people find this reassuring. On the other hand, where a method is based on experience, one finds much more concern with what to do about a situation than with putative explanations. With growing experience people develop rules of thumb and make generalisations.

The function of the staff is entirely different in the two situations, but it is interesting that they tend to be regarded with considerable respect in either case.

(g) ROLES AND TASKS

Palmer and Low use the term role freely, Adair makes only passing references to roles, but the other two authors do not use the term. Palmer writes that one of his aims is to help group members to carry out better the roles they may find themselves in subsequently. Low writes of the importance of members of staff differentiating clearly between different roles they take at different stages and so emphasising from the start 'the relationship between clarity of roles and organisational effectiveness'.

The term 'role' carries persistent undertones due to its origin. A role in the dramatic setting is acted or played, it is taken on temporarily and can be dropped. It may be suggested that the authors who do not make use of the term are more concerned with lasting developments in people and their relationship than with the adoption or setting up of temporary patterns of behaviour.

The authors clearly differ as to what may be regarded as a task. The Coverdale definition for instance is very specific and elaborate. For Waterston and Adair groups have tasks to carry out. For both of them tasks involve things to be done. Plans have to be made and group members' skills turned to account. Not all tasks are suitable; for instance Adair rejected 'group introspection' as a task for military groups. In Palmer's account the task of the group is to study its own behaviour as a group as it happens. Low adopts an intermediate position, distinguishing between tasks and process-tasks, his process-task being the same as Palmer's task.

It is worth considering two distinct ways of studying the operation of a group. One way of doing so is to observe the relationships exhibited between the members. As the pattern of relationships develops and as our appreciation of these patterns grows, we can see that in some sense we are studying the structure of the group. It would be useful if we could find a suitable phrase for behaving in terms of the pattern of relationships that evolves for each member out of their interactions with others. 'Implementing a role' would come near to supplying such a phrase, if the word 'role' could shed the undertones of acting a part.

A second way of studying a group is to observe it carrying out tasks, to see how in doing so objectives are set, plans are made, and how these plans are effective if they specify what each person does, when and where. In group activities of any complexity, a plan for a number of people must take account of their interactions; thus efficient planning will lead to operating in terms of relationships between people as well as specifying things for each to do. Turning back now to the earlier treatment in terms of structure it can be seen that knowledge and even understanding of the structure is not enough for the carrying out of a task; a plan which indicates what each member is to do when and where is also needed.

The point of this discussion is that one may begin either by being concerned with structure of a group, i.e. the pattern of relationships among members, or one may start with function, i.e. what each member is to do; but in either case, if one goes far enough towards producing an effective plan for a job, the other aspect of the group must be taken into account. The two approaches can then be seen to be complementary and neither alone gives a complete picture of a group in action.

This conclusion, that the balance of structure and function is required for a complete picture, highlights certain weaknesses in the methods as described by the authors.

Many participants will proceed from courses such as those described by Low and Palmer to join groups with genuine work to do. How appropriate is the emphasis on studying behaviour, in the absence of a task, to promoting the effective carrying out of jobs of work?

On the other hand Waterston quotes an earlier article by Roche and Waterston[2] that 'The human and emotional issues which arise when people do things together—which is the work situation—are different from those which arise when people merely talk together about what they might do in hypothetical circumstances'. He does not go on to develop the theme that 'the human and emotional issues which arise when people do things together' are those generated in doing what they are doing, and that they will not be the same if the thing to be done is to classify the advertisements in a newspaper or if it is to defuse a bomb! It is legitimate to ask whether coping with the human and emotional issues arising on courses equips one to tackle, say, real competition with a colleague or with the real risk of losing a job, or the risk of making an enemy of a director by obstructing his favourite scheme. The Coverdale method is designed to produce co-operation, thereby reducing conflict, and pays much attention to success, which when done sensibly builds morale. The results of this method can be very rewarding. It would seem, however, that emphasis on co-operation and on studying success could mean that difficulties arising from, say, personal animosities or conflict of aims were left unstudied. Thus participants could leave courses insufficiently apprised of the nature of such difficulties or of methods to adopt should they be encountered.

(h) USE OF TERMS

I have said something about different usages of 'task' and 'process'. Differences in the use of terms can obscure similarities between methods. For instance, Palmer's theoretical assumption (e) involves the *open systems* approach. An organisation or group may operate as if within a *closed system* implying it is independent of its environment or may operate always with recognition of environmental influences, in other words as *an open system*. Low and Bridger are certainly alive to this distinction; they too show the influence of the environmental factors which, though not apparent in proceedings of the group, can be brought to light.

An important influence in the development of Coverdale methods was the view that, in business in particular, many *situations are 'open'* in the sense that full information, to allow them to be treated as *closed situations* capable of a solution, could never become available. In such an open situation, however, action of some kind may be necessary. Groups are therefore encouraged to take action and do something in open situations.

The term 'open system' is not the same as 'open situation'; but both terms seem to relate to situations where action is called for in an environment that is changeable and is not fully amenable to control.

An important example of a 'closed situation' is where a student is given a 'case study' to work on, for the information contained in the folder he has been handed is the sum total of information available to him. Would it not follow that a group dealing with such a case study would be, in Palmer's sense, operating as a closed system?

Inevitably we find words that are not used to mean the same by all the authors. Could one expect terms like leadership, conflict or support to mean the same where there is a background of psychoanalytic theory, as they do where there is not?

(i) METHODS OF OPERATION

In addition to differences in the content of the five methods there are also differences in the ways the methods are operated. In all of them a member of staff is attached to a group of participants, and in each the staff member's job is to help the group. The amount of information the authors give us about these members of staff varies, but there is enough to show that some points of importance are involved.

Marcus gives in some detail the training that the group leaders (who are prison officers) undergo and it is clear that as leaders they have to be very patient with their groups and to accept behaviour and language incompatible with their normal idea of prison. We are not told about the methods of those that train them, but we learn that the prison officers do tend to become committed to the work, to accept the new climate and to adopt an attitude of responsibility for those inmates who form their group.

Low tells us something of the training and selection of staff members; readers may feel it is unfortunate that Palmer and Waterston tell us little about this side of the training. The evidence of Adair's account is that those who conduct his groups do not receive (or require) extensive training and that their chief function is to see that a programme is carried through.

The reader may have noted that the term used for the member of staff associated with a group varies from one method to another. Thus a group may have a 'leader', a 'tutor', a 'consultant' or a 'coach'; or, going outside the methods described here, terms include 'trainer', 'conductor', 'resource', 'facilitator', and 'change agent'. A trainer may be expected to be working to produce a known product, a coach to be concerned to help those in the group to improve their performance, consultants to give advice from their store of experience. The term 'change agent' may suggest someone deliberately attempting to be neutral, while letting you know what is expected. All these terms have been chosen with care by their users, but the implications of the various terms may be different for participants and lead to frustrations likely to be reflected in the relations that develop. Such differences in relations can be enhanced by organisational differences, such as whether the staff member behaves as a member of the group or not, by whether the staff members segregate themselves at meals, or whether staff members are available for technical discussion or to meet socially outside the session times.

The method of inducing groups to make discoveries by intervening for the most part with questions can be very unsettling, but so can be the method of never answering questions or appeals for help directly. Whereas in Palmer's account one function of his consultant is to embody authority, it is relevant to ask whether the mode adopted for exercising authority, as in the extract from the proceedings of a group, is one which the staff would recommend participants to imitate in normal social situations.

There are differences between, on the one hand, situations (e.g. Low and Palmer) where vestiges of psychoanalytic methods survive, and progress is sought by the offer of theory-based explanations and their ultimate incorporation by the participants; and on the other where, as in the Coverdale method, the function of a coach is to help a group to discover for itself some practical method which enables members of a group to co-operate and make progress in whatever job is in hand. Thus, while a relationship of trust and mutual respect usually develops between the members of a group and the member of staff attached, the quality of this relationship will be special to the method in use.

In the five chapters there are references to effects that staff members can produce or encourage in groups, but little if any weight is given to the effects of a staff member's own performance on the process in groups and on the subsequent behaviour of participants. The authors do not say what steps they take to study the 'process' effects of their own performance on the participants, or indeed whether they check that what they do themselves, and how they do it, can usefully be taken as an example to be followed.

(j) SUMMARY OF COMPARISONS

Comparisons have been made above between the five methods with respect to a number of important features. If these are set out in tabular form, it becomes somewhat easier to see the relationships between the methods and the extent to which concepts or practices found in them are unique.

(a)	The concept of a group	as a unit Low, Palmer	as a team Waterston, Adair	as a number of individuals Marcus
(b)	Usual size of small group	5–8 Waterston, Adair	9–15 Palmer, Low Marcus?	
(c)	The composition	all look for heterogeneity		
(d)	Process and content	emphasis on process Palmer, Marcus	emphasis on process and content Low, Adair	emphasis on content Waterston
(e)	Hidden agenda, types i–iv	use all types (i–iv) Marcus, Low, Palmer	Adair?	not using type iv Waterston
(f)	Theory and experience	emphasis on theory Marcus, Low, Palmer	emphasis on history Adair	emphasis on experience Waterston
(g)	Role and job	emphasis on roles Palmer	Low Marcus? Adair	emphasis on jobs Waterston

(h) and (i) do not lend themselves to tabular form.

On the basis of this very rough classification (which would not necessarily be accepted by the authors and which has been affected in some cases by what authors have chosen to say or not say) very few characteristics are in fact unique to any method. One could probably say that the pattern of characteristics was in each case unique.

Low and Palmer are usually in the same bracket, the most notable exception being Low's concern with doing a job, and in most cases they differ markedly from Waterston. Adair is in several respects closer to Waterston than to Low and Palmer. Marcus is often difficult to place but on the whole tends to be like Low and Palmer.

The results of this process of comparison are compatible with the view put forward later that all the methods have their uses. Anyone wishing to use one should work out, with the practitioner concerned, the benefits sought and the means by which they will try to obtain them.

Section 3: Insight, Transfer and Applications

Two beliefs are found in all the methods. The first is that learning by discovery means better learning and the second, which is crucial for them, that what is learnt in training groups is transferred to situations outside the training groups.

Learning by discovery implies moments of insight. Psychologists talk of an 'aha' experience as a concomitant of insight. This is a recognisable personal experience, often accompanied by some overt sign or behaviour and often long remembered. The content of the insight, the discovery, may be anything, such as seeing a new way of tying up parcels, or that if the last two digits of a number are divisible by four so also is the number as a whole, or realising that one has been tactless.

The psychological reality of the experience of 'aha' is, however, no guarantee that the intellectual content will stand up to the processes of reasoning; the content may be mistaken or misleading.

Another point to remember about learning by discovery is that it can be very time-consuming and frustrating, for no one can tell how long it will take to make a discovery.

Transfer is used in two senses. In one sense of the word, transfer occurs when some concept or discovery is carried over from one situation to another, as when a method found to be useful in a group in a course for managers is applied say in a family group or in a Parochial Church Council. Such transfer will only be useful when circumstances are sufficiently similar, and great differences exist between people in their ability to judge what is sufficiently similar.

Transfer in the second sense of transferring a usable skill takes longer before it is practicable.

When, after some discovery in a training situation, a procedure has been developed in a group (such as of asking questions to ensure that all present understand some particular point, or of appointing someone to be secretary to the group) it may be transferred as a ritual and used elsewhere with or without relevance. A step towards increased usefulness is made when 'what was ritual becomes meaningful' (a stage which itself involves insight). When this change occurs reasons can then be given for the course of action adopted (e.g. that, by having a secretary, a record of proceedings can be ensured and that information about actions delegated can be assembled and collated). Even then, however, the implementation of the procedure may prove to be too hard or too complicated for participants, till planning and repeated practice have led to the development of expertise. Thus transfer, in the sense of applying some skill in a fresh situation, cannot occur till the time spent in the development of the skill has elapsed.

(A somewhat similar line of reasoning can be applied to claims made for work in small groups, that barriers between people can be broken down and their potential realised. Potential energy as such does nothing, energy misapplied or inadequately controlled can be destructive; only by planning, trial and practice can potential energy released in small groups be brought under control and be put to useful work, and of course this, too, takes time.)

An aspect of transfer that is little touched on in the chapters is the difficulty that participants meet when they return to a setting in which few or none of their colleagues have had similar experience. Not only is there a language difficulty of explaining to others ideas newly acquired in terms that will be understood, but also, since they have only recently acquired them and had little opportunity of practising, they will have difficulty in expounding them. It may even be difficult for beginners to maintain their enthusiasm in the face of indifference, let alone personal plans or procedure that might flourish in a climate of understanding and good will. Thus there can be great inefficiency resulting from the introduction of new methods (and this can apply to any method of training) when there is inadequate preparation for their introduction and use.

Another difference affecting transfer separates on the one hand Palmer, Low and Marcus, in whose methods the changes resulting are largely changes of outlook and attitude, from Coverdale training on the other hand where the chief changes talked about are in overt behaviour. Adair's work does not fall easily into either category. This difference leads to the question whether the value of small group work lies in it being a matrix for an experience from which participants emerge looking at themselves and their relationships with other people in a new light; or whether its value is in providing a convenient teaching milieu for participants to learn new and useful techniques and procedures.

It is not clear whether the two approaches are divergent, representing two distinct routes for making progress, or whether each is incomplete in the sense that concentration on either would in the long run reveal how necessary the other was becoming. For, if a changed outlook be regarded as an end product, the question remains open as to what are the practical effects of such a change. When, however, emphasis is on learning new techniques for interaction with other people, behavioural changes can turn out to be no more than rituals, with no basis of understanding or even, in the worst case, to be ploys deliberately adopted by someone who has concealed aims of his own. The implication is that change of outlook and change of behaviour must develop together.

Section 4: Model and Metaphor

Several of the authors refer to an 'import–conversion–export' model for what goes on in groups; but insofar as the five methods are concerned with helping participants to learn and develop in various ways, greater emphasis on growth rather than change is called for. This suggests that a different metaphor which emphasised growth would be more helpful. Suppose we turn to an activity that is essentially concerned with growth, for example, agriculture. We could then say that, metaphorically, each method deals with a different crop, different crops are best suited by different climates and the processes of husbandry will differ from one to another. The important implications for small group training are, first, that when a new crop is to be introduced and established the nature of the product must be made known; in other words, when a new method of training is proposed there must be a reasonable or at least a plausible account of what it is designed to achieve. Just as plants that flourish but bear no fruit may yet be recognised as useful for making windbreaks or for giving shade, or providing colour or beautiful flowers at certain seasons, so training may produce desirable effects other than an immediate financial return. Secondly even the most expert husbandry will not lead to a good crop if the climate is altogether unfavourable, something that should be considered before any work is undertaken. Thirdly, planting or sowing are seldom enough by themselves to ensure a good crop; they need to be supplemented by cultivation. In terms of small groups this suggests that active intervention is desirable after the initial experience. Asking questions later is not enough, further interaction between the practitioners and participants is required to enhance or ensure growth. The appropriate form of intervention may well be different for different methods of training.

As Farrell points out in his commentary, Palmer seems little concerned with what participants do after a course (though he mentions that some came back to other courses); he points out that Low and Adair show some interest, while Coverdale makes express provision for further contact with participants after courses, to confirm and enhance what has been learnt. Marcus describes a somewhat different situation, in which support for the group leaders continues long after the meetings of their initiatory training and over the period when they are putting what they have learnt into effect in leading their groups of inmates.

As with growing crops, it may be some considerable time before a product is harvested or any benefit realised. One can, of course, look for signs of progress and an obvious question is whether examples can be given of recognisable stages of development.

It seems possible to identify some from Waterston's and from Low's accounts, and to hazard guesses at such stages in what Marcus and Adair have written.

Thus, for instance, it is not unusual in a Coverdale course to find business men being indignant, at an early stage, at being invited to carry out some 'simple task'. It is a distinct sign of progress when such a group realises that important lessons can be learned from simple operations, for example that confusion can result when there are undiscovered differences as to the aim of an exercise. Similar is the discovery that, in training, tasks can be vehicles for learning about co-operation, though not important in themselves. Another sign of progress is to recognise that it gives valuable experience to be, for a time, an observer of the activities of other members of the group. The developmental stages one can see in Low's account are different, such as understanding the role of the consultant, and recognising the value of taking time off to review. There is also the important recognition that others have little power to help you in your private concerns, but that members of a group can help one another when they are dealing with matters of which they have experience in common, whence his emphasis on dealing with the 'here and now'.

Palmer, though he speaks of stages, does not describe any. Coming to terms with the role of the consultant seems to be one. Appreciation by a group member of how he is seen by his fellows, or that the consultant can help him to appreciate the likely origin of some of his behaviour seem to be others.

Beyond such fairly general signs, experienced members of staff will indubitably notice and come to look for others, to help them to appraise the ways things are going, and as pointers to what to do and to look for next.

One should remember incidentally that, though participants are usually keen to know about their own progress, they may not recognise as progress what a member of staff sees as such.

Many signs can be indicators of progress, though quite inappropriate as criteria to work to. Sometimes such an indicator takes the form of spontaneous use by a participant of technical terms or phrases, such as 'the group needs help since it is engaged in S-activity', or 'let us pay more attention to listening and support' or 'I now see how I can contribute to team maintenance'. In such a case Farrell's admonition about WOT and the consultant's readiness to use it as evidence of progress is very much to the point. If the words used can be compared with actions and the two are found not to match, the appearance of progress is illusory. If, however, words and acts are found to be coherent with one another, then the words are not mere jargon. It is in this area that Farrell's points about a 'WOT' and the consultant's readiness to interpret the use of it as evidence of progress are so important.

Section 5:
What has been achieved and has it been worthwhile?

As already emphasised, there is a considerable volume of literature about small group methods. The bulk of it is about T-groups and sensitivity training. Reference to this literature shows that there has been great difficulty in establishing what are the effects of T-groups. In itself this may not be too serious for present purposes, because none of the five authors admits that they work with T-groups or sensitivity training; but relatively very little has been written about the effects of other methods.

It has been said that, in respect to T-groups, the difficulties of appraisal of effects are largely methodological and also that the existing classification of observations, for treatment by current statistical methods, destroys the richness of the phenomena. The case is similar here. The references by the five authors to effects of their work are very varied (e.g. effects such as reappearance in later training courses, improved marital relations, a better safety record at a refinery, or better methods of car-parking) and no simple set of categories may be adequate to describe them.

In one respect the Coverdale method goes further for it inculcates self-monitoring and encourages participants, after taking part in a course of this kind, to set themselves their own standards and their own objectives, and to determine for themselves whether these are reached (e.g. they may plan to reduce the length of committee meetings and to ensure that decisions are implemented). Thus it should become automatic that what is achieved is appraised and any lessons taken into account for the future.

In his chapter, Waterston indicates that the Coverdale organisation applies these methods to its own work with clients and he also quotes reports from clients telling how they have found they benefited from applying what they had learnt. This method is valuable where meaningful objectives can be specified in advance.

Though interesting and varied, the evidence offered cannot be described as conclusive or even impressive in a statistical sense; as it stands it is probably more useful as evidence of the authors' attitudes to this matter than as material for readers to judge by. The fashionable emphasis on statistics and a quantitative approach, however, ensures that much potentially valuable evidence is never collected.

The alternative of studying the phenomena in detail, so as to distinguish the important kinds of event or influence, seems to be dismissed as anecdotal by some writers (e.g. D. Stack,[3] and J. N. Campbell and M. D. Dunnette[4]). But nothing is so useful with material so uncontrolled as the proceedings of small groups as to collect and record observations of events and, where available, anecdotes.

The value of anecdote at this stage is much too readily discounted. I have often noticed the lack of facility shown by even experienced observers in recalling events or incidents; anecdotes have great merits, being more readily recalled and likely to start fresh lines of thought. But, as the number of relevant anecdotes increases, it becomes more and more difficult to comprehend what the information in them amounts to. So they need to be sorted and compared till similarities and differences are noticed. Thence one can move by way of groupings and distinctions to categories and generalisations. As generalisations are made, an important change takes place, for happenings cease to be incidents and can be treated as 'instances' of this or that generalisation. Instances can be counted, and this is where what is usually accepted as statistical treatment begins.

Instances of effects, such as those given by Waterston (or by Palmer), are open to the criticism that no one can prove they would not have taken place without the training. There is little doubt, however, that those who made the reports believed in the relevance of the training and attribute what they did and achieved in some measure to it. It becomes progressively more reasonable, as instances accumulate, to pay attention to them and the claims that accompany them.

The question of psychological upset to the individual is often raised. None of the authors would admit that there was any important incidence of undue stress. The fact that some participants find difficulty or come under stress in following a course of training is, in my submission, characteristic of any worthwhile endeavour. Clearly it is obligatory for practitioners to ensure, so far as they can, that stress or difficulty is resolved. The process is itself healthy. When people face and overcome difficulties and learn from doing so how to do so again, we may be sure that something valuable is in progress.

After collecting evidence on what has been achieved by the use of a method of training, there is another question to answer; 'Has it been worthwhile?'.

Once this question is asked, the field of enquiry suddenly expands from the content or style of courses and their after-effects to the transaction as a whole. At first sight the transaction is between practitioners and clients fulfilling some kind of contract, but neither of these classes is simple. For instance, some clients participate in courses themselves, many more sponsor others who do. Many participants consequently contribute their time and efforts but do not pay fees. However, where this is so someone else pays them. This is true of courses whether given in a prison (Chapter 4) or at Sandhurst (Chapter 1), it is as true of 'in-company' courses in a great organisation (Chapter 5) as of courses run by a non-profit making institute (Chapter 3) or by a commercial organisation (Chapter 2) that depends on profits from running them.

I have no doubt that the cost to a participant affects his attitude to what he receives but the evidence does not suggest a simple relationship between cost and either public esteem or effectiveness.

The situation that a practitioner is in, and so his standpoint, will vary depending on what kind of organisation he is working for and his terms of employment. Looked at thus the transaction as a whole will be different for each individual or organisation involved and must be judged by each from their own point of view.

Section 6

In this chapter I have drawn attention to similarities and differences among five methods. I have tried to show that in a number of important ways these small group methods *share* characteristics that are associated with the valuable properties that make small groups powerful and important.

After the euphoria of the early sixties, people came to realise that going on sensitivity training or T-groups was not a panacea for organisational ills. Over the past few years methods have been growing up that differ in interesting ways, and the questions 'for whom and for what are they useful?' become more relevant than whether they are of use at all.

The proportion of participants who benefit could be increased if more attention were given to matching between individuals and what is being offered. It could be, for instance, that different types of people, or people in different age ranges, or in different occupations, would be best suited by different methods, or again that some people would benefit from encountering more than one method. Advance in this direction might come about if independent advice were sought (and available), or even if practitioners of different methods were prepared to co-operate in this respect.

It has become clearer that the experience of being a member of a small group is not in itself enough. Participants must understand that such an experience is only the start of a learning process. It will depend on them whether they have the persistence to make good use of what has been begun. As with any skill, practice and practice is called for.

I am advocating a pragmatic view that there is reasonable evidence for the usefulness of these methods and that what are now needed most are means of ensuring that they are employed to best advantage. People who knew enough and had had enough experience of the various methods to be able to give sound advice would be most valuable. Whether such people will be training officers, or independent consultants, or experts from academic circles remains to be seen. They will need to be able to help individuals and organisations to understand what are the likely effects of embarking on this or that method and what acquaintance with the method will enable participants to achieve, and so be equipped to judge for themselves whether the effort and expenditure envisaged are likely to be worthwhile.

References

1. Homan, G. C. *The Human Group* (1950) New York: Harcourt Brace.
2. Roche, S. G.; Waterston, J. 'Coverdale Training: Building on Ability', *Training and Development Journal* (1972), Feb , p. 47, American Society for Training and Development Inc.
3. Stack D. 'Survey of Research on T-Groups', *T-Group theory and laboratory practice* (1965), Ed. Bradtord Gibb and Benne.
4. Campbell, J. N. and Dunnette, M. D. 'Effectiveness of T-Group Experiences in Managerial Training Development', *Psychol. Bull.* (1968), vol. 70, pp. 73–104.

© 1979 B. Babington Smith.

Postscripts

OCTOBER 1978

CHAPTER 1   DR. J. E. ADAIR

Though this chapter was completed two or three years ago, the author finds that it still represents his position so far as principles are concerned.

CHAPTER 2   A. D. SHARP (FOR J. WATERSTON)

Since the chapter on Coverdale Training was written the methods described have continued to be found useful by an ever-increasing number of people in a widening variety of situations. Approximately 5,000 delegates per year now attend courses, a number of which are run outside the United Kingdom, some in languages other than English.

The main features of the method remain unchanged, as do the underlying themes. These of course have never been regarded by Coverdale consultants as 'scientific truths' but rather as descriptive categories into which delegates find it helpful to group the lessons which they derive from the experience. Perhaps the only major feature of the small-group work to which, in the light of subsequent experience, we give more emphasis than is apparent in the chapter, is to centre the Part I course experience on deliberate team formation. Delegates are thus invited from the start to look outwards from themselves at what they can contribute to help.

The primary concern of The Coverdale Organisation and the consultants who comprise it, as was that of Ralph Coverdale, remains one of ensuring that what is provided is useful. This concern, coupled with a substantial increase in the amount of organisation development work in very large organisations, has meant that a major concentration in recent years has been on trying to ensure that lessons gained from the courses by individuals are applied, built upon and extended at work—i.e. in installing progressive learning from experience throughout organisations. However, the small-group training courses have remained an essential starting point in the total approach. The experience of both Coverdale consultants and the client organisations concerned is that individuals can be helped by these means to begin to set up habits and ways of working which enable them to become more effective as individuals, in groups and in organisations. Obviously once their development is under way its extent depends on their own efforts.

CHAPTER 3 B. W. M. PALMER

(a) Since this paper was written the Centre for Applied Social Research has ceased to exist as a distinct unit within the Tavistock Institute. The group relations training programme has continued under the joint directorship of E. J. Miller and W. G. Lawrence. P. M. Turquet was tragically killed in a road accident in 1975.

(b) The account of W-activity and S-activity in this paper now appears unsatisfactory. It is important to distinguish between the types of individual mental activity, which Freud referred to as secondary process and primary process, to which the above terms correspond, and the manifestations of mind in the social system of the group, which Bion termed work group activity and basic assumption activity.

(c) Readers are also referred to these more recent studies:

Bazalgette, J. L. 'School Life and Work Life—A Study of Transition in the Inner City', Hutchinson, 1978.

Colman, A. D. and Beston, W. H. (eds) 'Group Relations Reader', The A. K. Rice Institute, 1975.

Hutton, J. M., Quine, C. and Reed, B. D. 'The Wholeness of Life', YMCA, 1976.

Lawrence, W. G. (ed) 'Exploring Individual and Organisational Boundaries', John Wiley (in press).

Palmer, B. W. M. 'Fantasy and Reality in Group Life: A Model for Learning by Experience', in N. McCaughan (ed), 'Group Work: Learning and Practice', Allen & Unwin, 1978.

Reed, B. D. 'The Dynamics of Religion', Darton, Longman and Todd, 1978.

Reed, B. D. 'Organisational Role Analysis' in C. L. Cooper (ed), 'Developing Social Skills in Managers', Macmillan, 1976.

Reed, B. D., Hutton, J. M., and Bazalgette, J. L. 'Freedom to Study', Overseas Students Trust, 1978.

CHAPTER 4 B. MARCUS

Naturally, considerable changes have taken place since the above chapter was originally composed. The therapeutic community ideology has been consolidated, so that it becomes a meaningless exercise to separate out the small group work from the matrix in which it has been embedded. Nevertheless the following modifications should be noted:

1. Like the whole of the prison service, Grendon has suffered from staff shortages. This has led to some pruning in the staff training programme. But a compensating process has been a greater confidence in the institution's ethos, which in turn has led to training and support for group leaders being given 'locally', i.e. at wing levels: this tends to encroach on the functions of the more centralised training described above.
2. The expansion of the role of group officer to that of general therapeutic agent has proceeded apace.
3. It is not, by and large, possible to sustain the claim that Grendon reduces reconviction rates, although the possibility of Grendon ac-

cepting a poor risk population is not ruled out. Very recently Gunn *et al*[1] have questioned the relevance of using reconviction statistics as a criterion for success in an institution of this kind.
4. Evidence has accumulated to show that Grendon admits, in relation to the general prison population, a very high proportion of violent offenders, yet deals with this population with a comparatively small amount of disciplinary troubles. This is interpreted as good objective evidence for the high level of inter-personal relationships which most observers subjectively feel, and which is the strongest argument for the regime.
5. There are now six wings, all group-orientated.

REFERENCE

1. Gunn, J., Robertson G., Dell, S., Way, C., Psychiatric Aspects of Imprisonment, Academic Press 1978 (p. 166 *et seq.*).

CHAPTER 5   K. B. LOW (FOR LOW AND BRIDGER)

A review of what has been achieved since the 'Practice of Management' courses began reveals two important and complementary emphases, which are relevant to the management of organisations in general.

Evidence from the courses, which now form an integral part of a total management development programme, including the application of group dynamics learning to a business game, shows that each individual manager can take a particular lesson for himself from his experiences. For some, who may work in organisations where emphasis on collaboration in groups is not particularly relevant or strong, the main lesson may well be about the need to strengthen individual skills or knowledge in order to work more effectively as managers. For others the lesson can be about the value of 'temporary systems', such as project teams, or new forms of matrix organisation; in such cases a heightened awareness of group dynamics can be the starting point for change and for action. It is obvious, therefore, that selection for course membership must be a carefully considered process, involving the participant, his own manager and the course organiser. Experience demonstrates increasingly the value of a participant being able to link the lessons from the course to his own particular situation at work and as a member of a wider society beyond.

The 'network' of people which has been created as a result of the 'Practice of Management' is now seen not as a 'group-within-a-group', believed by outsiders to possess esoteric or even threatening powers, but more as a loose collection of managers whose way of thinking is common and who are capable of acting almost automatically in ways based on similar values. These values are essentially those which respect the twin emphases of individuality and group cohesion. Thus the setting up of work teams, discussion groups or interviews with individuals is informed by the awareness drawn from the 'Practice of Management' of the delicate balance between personal objectives and desires and the sometimes competing and conflicting demands placed upon one by group activity.

It is the awareness of this balance which is perhaps the most significant outcome that a course participant can hope to grasp.

Name Index

Italic figures indicate names in references

Adair, J. E.   xi, 3, 85, 88, 103, 104, 105–8, 111–12, 121, 124
Adair *et al.*   105–8, 111–12, 114, 116, 118, 119, 121–2, 124, 125, 127, 128
A. K. Rice Institute   43
Allport, G. W.   *18*

Babington Smith, B.   xi, xii, 21, 23
Bales, R. F.   1, *4*
Barton, R.   65, *82*
Bazalgette, J. L.   61, *134*
Bednar, R. L.   *115*
Beston, W. H.   *134*
Bethel, Maine   2
Bion, W. R.   2, *4*, 43, 44–5, 47, 49, 55, *60*, 85, 87, *134*
Bird, C.   *18*
Blake, R. R.   *115*
Borgatta, E.   1, *4*
Bowlby, J.   46, *60*
Bradford, Leland   2
Bridger, H.   xi, xii

California Department of Correction   74
Campbell, J. N.   130, *132*
C.A.S.R. (Centre for Applied Social Research)   41, 58, *134*
Churchill, Winston   7
Colman, A. D.   *134*
Coverdale, R.   xi, 3, 20, 21, 23, 35, 40, 85, 106, 110, 133
Crowcroft, A.   *60*

Dartmoor Prison   76
Dell, S.   *135*
Department of Employment   37
Dunnette, M. D.   130, *132*

East, W. N.   *82*
Eastbourne Conference   83–4
Emery, F. E.   *60*
Esso Petroleum Company Ltd.   23

Farrell, B. A.   xi, xii, *115*, 128, 129
Fenton, N.   74, *82*
Food and Agriculture Organisation   37
Freud, S.   134

Goffman, E.   65, *82*
Gosling, R.   *61*
Great Britain   1, 2, 3, 7
Grendon Prison   62–82, 104, 113
Grubb Institute of Behavioural Studies   41, 43, 58, 103, 104
Gunn, J.   *135*
Gwynne, C.   *61*

Hare, P. A.   1, *4*
Harris, Henry   10, 11
Heller, F. A.   *18*
Herrick, R. W.   43
Herzberg, F.   101
Hickey, P.   *82*
Homan, G. C.   116, *132*
Hubert, W. H. de B.   *82*
Hull, G. J.   *82*
Hutchinson, D. G.   83
Hutton, Jean   43
Hutton, J. M.   *134*

India   1
Industrial Society   5, 14, 15

Japan   1
Jenkins, W. A.   *18*
Jones, Maxwell   2, *4*, 64, 65, *82*

NAME INDEX

Klein, M.   44, *60*

Laing, R. D.   46, *60*
Lawlis, G. F.   *115*
Lawrence, W. G.   *134*
Lewin, K.   1, 2, *4*, 5, 44
Low, K. B.   xii, 3, 103, 104, 106
Low, K. B., and Bridger, H.   3, 103, 104, 106, 108, 111, 116–22, 124, 125, 127, 128, 135
Luft, Dr. J.   102

McGregor, D. M.   101
Main, T. F.   2, *4*
Marcus, B.   xi, 4, *82*, 88, 103, 104, 113, 116, 117, 118, 119, 120, 121, 124, 125, 127, 128
Miles, M.   84
Miller, D. H.   *60*
Miller, E. J.   43, *60*, *61*, 134
Montgomery, Field Marshal Lord   16
Mouton, Jane S.   *115*

N.T.L. (National Training Laboratories)   2, 3, 43
Newton, M.   *82*
Northfields Military Hospital   2

Odbert, N. S.   *18*
Oxford Prison   63

Palmer, B. W. M.   3, 53, *61*, 103, 104, 106, 109–12, 116–21, 123, 124
Peck, Gregory   13
Pentonville Prison   76

Quine, C.   *134*

Reed, B. D.   43, *61*, *134*
Rice, A. K.   3, *4*, 41, 43, 47, 57, 58, *60*, *61*
Rice, Denis   43
Richardson, E.   43, *61*
Rickman, J.   2, *4*
Robertson, A.   66, *81*
Robertson, G.   *135*
Roche, S.   *40*, *132*

Sandhurst (R.M.C.)   3
Schmidt, W. H.   *18*
Sharp, A. D.   *133*
Slavson, S. R.   1, *4*
Smith, P. B.   *61*
Sofer, C.   *60*
South Africa   1
Stack, D.   130, *132*
Steel Company of Wales   20
Strachey, J.   44, *60*
Sutherland, J. D.   *61*

Tannenbaum, R.   *18*
The Coverdale Organisation   40, *133*
T.I.H.R. (Tavistock Institute of Human Relations)   2, 41, 42, 43
Trist, E. L.   *60*, *61*, 84
Turquet, P. M.   xi, xii, 41, 44, 57, *61*, 134

University of Bristol   41
University of Leicester   42
U.S.A.   1, 3

Waterston, J.   3, 40, 104, 116–19, 121, 122, 124, 128, 130, *132*
Wates Ltd.   14
Way, C.   *135*
Winnicott, D. W.   54, *61*
Wittgenstein, L.   *114*
Woodhouse, D. L.   *61*

Subject Index

Accident Prevention 38
ACL (Action Centred Leadership) 5, 14–17, 103, 104, 105, 112
Action 21, 29, 59
Adair's trefoil model 9, 10, 104
'Aha' experience 126
Aims 99
　clarification of 28, 29, 111
　clarity of 3
　of medicine 110
　of psychiatry 110
　psychological 68
　setting 23
　sociological 68
Analysis, Field Force 94, 95
　Jungian 109
　protracted 22
　psycho- 110
Anecdotes, value of 130
Application of learning
　back at work 21, 126, 133
Appraisal 88, 129
　system 84
Assumptions 7, 25, 45, 48, 49, 65, 75, 78, 85
　basic (Bion) 45, 112
　medical 62
　need to change 25
　need to question 39
　practical 78
　practitioners, discussion of 104–10, 113, 114
　theoretical 44, 104, 117, 123
Attitudes
　changes in 39, 59, 104
Authority
　and leadership 44, 105
　exercise of 124
　from mere status 88
　nature of 44
　participative 75
　personal 88
　problems of 70

process and task 33
reprimanding 51
severe 52
see also Leadership
Awareness 58, 105
　of difficulties 22

Behaviour 124, 131
　Bion's theory of 43, 44, 45
　change of 39, 127
　supportive 22, 32

Case studies 25, 97, 123
　see also Open or closed
Cause–effect relationships affecting courses 100
Changes
　duration of 57
　in area of insight 57, 59
　in attitude 38, 104
　in behaviour 38, 77, 101, 127
　in course members 6
　of job 60
　organisational 59
Clarification 29, 59, 60, 103
Closed-system, etc. 44, 46, 123
　see also Open or closed
Coach see under Operator
Common comprehension 30
　languages 116
　way of thinking 135
Communalism 64
Confidentiality 22, 25, 78, 79, 116
Conflict 3, 95, 123
　of loyalties 51, 53, 94
Confrontation
　reality 76
Consultant see under Operator
Content and process 48, 84, 86, 90, 93, 98, 101
Co-operation 33, 34

139

SUBJECT INDEX

Courses
 design of 6, 36, 88, 89
 membership of 42
 nomination to 89
 residential 89, 92–6
 selection for 131
 and Universities 114
Coverdale courses 24, 25, 30–6, 103, 128
Criteria
 how shall we know . . . ? 29
 of progress or success 30, 68, 129
Custodialism 64

Deciding 55
Decision making 10, 46, 64, 75, 90, 91, 95, 99
Dependence 47, 87
De-skilling 72, 79
Development
 of skill, takes time 126
 of understanding 19
 stages of 128, 129
 see also under Organisation
Discovery 4, 124
Disinterestedness 15, 105

Educational device 119
Educational enterprise 114
Enthusiasm 3, 116
Euphoria 3
Evaluation 11, 35, 57, 76, 79, 100–1, 111, 114, 129–32
 studies 37–40
 see also Appraisal; Monitoring
Expectancy 47
Experience in common 116
 and generalisations 121
 and theory 121
Experiential learning 20–26, 85–6, 100

Fantasy 48, 51–3, 56
Fees, relevance of 111, 131
Feedback 78, 84, 87, 88
 see also Review
Fight-flight 47, 48
'Fishbowl' exercise 94
Follow up 38, 39, 58, 97, 101, 112, 128
Function 13, 46, 122

Generalisation 105, 106, 130
'Gestalt' xii

Getting to know people 116, 118
'Good enough'
 environment 54
 shared experience 99
'Grassing' 77, 78
Group
 aims 99
 behaviour 87
 with a boundary 50, 75
 common interest 42, 92, 96
 composition of 118
 consultation 93
 control 80, 112
 counselling 74
 culture 85
 decisions 117
 discussion 90, 95
 dynamics 1, 5, 6, 11, 16, 95, 98, 135
 to be effective 87
 as an entity 85
 encounter xii
 functioning 84
 heterogeneous 93
 homogeneous 92, 96
 inter group events 42, 73, 74, 94
 large 42, 73
 leaderless 2, 42, 54, 87
 leaders 62, 71, 73, 124, 134
 maintenance 9, 87
 more than the sum of its parts 85
 nature of 93, 117
 power of 117
 as a powerful agent 111
 process 78, 87, 95, 101
 projects 102
 relations 42
 Small xi, 1, 2, 4, 5, 8, 12, 14, 17, 19, 33, 37, 41, 42, 48–57, 62–6, 68, 73, 74–6, 83, 92, 93, 96, 103, 107, 118
  behaviour of 85
  consultant contributions to 55, 56
  effects of 76
  growth of prestige 75
  how they function 96
  method of 1, 49, 53, 54, 74, 83, 103
  needs in life of 8
  organisation of 54, 55
  power of 1, 117, 131
  and psychotherapy 1
  work 54, 73, 75, 79, 84
 size 118
 structure 54, 122
 survival 45
 techniques 71, 72
 therapeutic 50

SUBJECT INDEX

T (or Training)   xi, 2, 3, 4, 6, 11, 16, 57, 86, 129, 131
  work   77, 90, 91, 93
  work, course   70
  worker, support for   71, 72
Growth   127, 128

Hawthorne
  effect   117
  experiment   117
'Here and now'   44, 55, 100, 117
Hidden agenda   86, 120-1, 125
  see also Unexpressed
Hierarchical barrier   65
Hostility   52-3

Indicators of
  improvement   68
  progress   129
Information   29, 30, 31
Insight   .19, 90, 95, 102, 104-8, 126
  see also under Changes
Instructions   25, 26
Intergroup exchanges   *see* Group
Interpersonal relations   *see* Relations
Interpretations
  by staff members   27, 44, 55, 121

Jelling   99

Knowledge 'of' or 'about'   6
  see also Insight
Korean War and brainwashing   6

Leaderless group
  see Group: leaderless
Leadership   3, 44
  capacity   87
  and followership   15
  functional   5, 8, 15
  permissive style   54
  qualities   7, 8, 10
  selection for   10
  situational   8, 86, 87
  styles of   55
  three elements of (Rice)   45
  traits   7
  in W-activity   46
  see also Authority

Learning
  assumptions about   48
  capacity for   86
  by discovery   93, 104, 126
  from experience   19, 23, 25, 36, 45, 85, 100
  for leadership   42
  by marriage of experience and ideas   49
  participant centred   88
  relevance of, for real situation   101
  from work groups   102
Listening
  and proposing   32

Maintenance
  group   87
  team   9, 87
Management
  development to meet change   83
  and front line staff   67
  styles   83
Manipulation   69, 92, 94, 98
Matrix organisation   135
Medical profession   110
Medical setting   62
Metaphor   127, 128
Methods, new, risk of wasting   126
Milieu therapy   1, 69
Models   46, 47, 63, 79, 127, 128
Monitoring   45, 130
Moral imperative   66
Motivation   64, 89, 90, 101
Mutual trust and confidence   21, 23
  self-confidence   21, 22

Needs   8
  see also Adair's trefoil model

Observation
  on courses   22, 31, 119
  as source of information   31
  at work   31
Observing member   24
OCTUs   10
Open or closed
  instructions   2, 25
  situations   123
  systems   44, 46, 123
Operation, method of   123, 124
Operators (includes staff)   104-17
  change agents   124

SUBJECT INDEX

Operators cont...
   coaches 26
   effect of interpretation 27
   interventions 27
   job 26, 27
   methods 27, 28
   use of questions 27, 124
conductors 124
consultants
   active participants 56
   assignment to groups 91
   concern only for group development 99
   contributions 42
   dealing with questions 96, 99
   exercising leadership 56
   have to earn trust 99
   interpretations 55
   interventions 98
   learning the role 55
   relations to groups 98
   roles 97ff.
   seen as embodying authority 52, 53
   task of 55
   as teachers 86
   use of theories 55
co-trainers 91
course staff
   effects of behaviour 100, 124, 125
   meetings 91
   methods of selection 90
   roles, clarity of 98
   teaching and administrative roles 91
facilitator 124
front line staff 65, 67
group officers as facilitating agents 75
group leaders 74, 124
group operators 107–11
   leaders 124
   problems 71
   workers 124
resources 124
trainees 57, 91
trainers 6, 124
tutor 124
see also Practitioners

Organisation
   defensive use of 48
   strategies 33
Organisation–Development (O.D.) 34, 88, 97, 100, 109, 133

Participants
   course members, can become trainee consultants 91
      by being sent 100
      by invitation 89
      by nomination 60, 89
      by recruitment 42
      by selection 135
   course members
      range of 5, 14, 17, 19, 42, 43, 69–71, 96
      roles 56, 90
   group members, roles 56
   patients as active participants in therapy 65
   prison inmates 62–82
   prison officers 62–82
Penal problems
   approaches to 62
Permissiveness 64, 65, 66
Physical activity, effects of 21
Planning 23, 26, 30, 119
   co-operation to mutual benefit 31
Post course phase 96, 97
'Practice of management' course 84, 88–9, 101–2, 103, 119
Practitioners xi, 3, 131, 132
Preparation–action–review to improve 19, 24
Principles and practices
   based on experience 24, 90
   generalisations 27
   grouped together under themes 28–33
   that work 24
Prison culture 64–8, 76–80, 103, 113
   see also Participants
Problem solving 30, 88
Procedure, commonly understood and agreed 30
Process and content 86, 95, 98, 113, 122, 125
   awareness 100
   primary and secondary 134
Propaganda 111
Psychiatry 110, 111
Psychoanalysis 110
Psychoanalytic concepts 120, 123
Psychoanalytic methods 124
Psychological upset 126
Psychometric testing 64
Psychotherapy 2
Purpose 23, 25, 26

Realisation of potential 114, 126
Recidivism 63, 64, 68, 70, 81, 103, 113
Reconviction statistics 134–5
Reconvening a course 96, 97
Rehabilitation 64

SUBJECT INDEX

Relationships
  interpersonal 4
  patterns of 53, 122
  civilised patterns of 81, 135
  staff-participants 97–9
  between courses and 'back at work' 97
  between officers and inmates 69, 76, 77, 80, 81
  among prison inmates 80
Repression 120
Research 1, 57
Resource(s) 87, 90, 124
Responsibility 20, 91
Reviewing 24, 26, 94, 96
  to improve 30
Risks 24
  taking 88
Ritual 126
Role
  administrative 91
  clarity 91, 98
  concept of 86–7
  of consultants 55–6, 91, 97, 98, 119
  of course members 56
  dramatic performance 121
  implementation 122
  improvement 109
  performance 58, 103
  of staff members 91, 97–8, 102
  and task 121
  teaching 91

S-activity 45, 47–9, 51, 54–5, 56, 134
Selection
  course members 89, 91
  course staff 91
  by interview 10
Self-confidence 21
  evaluation 27
  monitoring 130
Sensitivity training 2, 105, 113
Situation
  open or closed 123
Skills
  process, interpersonal 32, 88, 102
  range in group 32
  recognition of 23, 32, 34
Social
  distance 64, 65, 69, 77
  inadequacy 63
  psychology 2
Sociology 2
Sociotechnical system 84, 102
'Something in it for . . .' 74

Staff
  see under Operators
Standards, concern for 120
Steering–working parties 34
Stress, psychological 131
Structure 93, 122
Success
  and confidence 23, 68,
  and morale 9, 22, 23, 122, 123
  and psychotherapy 68
  body of successful practices 24
  causes of 23
  emphasis on 23, 32, 122
  how to assess 68
Supervising for results 35
Support 28, 71, 92, 100
'Suspending business' 94, 99, 101
  see also Review
Synectics xii
Synthesis not compromise 28
Systems 46, 123
  small-plenary group 17
  socio-technical 84, 102
  temporary 88, 98, 100, 135
  see also 'Open or closed'
Systematic approach to getting things done 29, 30, 34

Task
  achievement 99
  performance 46
  preferred to case studies or discussion 25
  simple 26, 128
  as opposed to self-analysis 86
  as vehicle for learning 25, 128
  and process 119
  and role 121, 122
  see also Content
Teamwork 16, 37, 38, 103, 104, 117, 118, 133
Themes 19, 23, 28–33
Theoretical framework 44, 85, 104, 106, 107
Theory
  Bion's, of small group behaviour 43–5
  and experience 21, 121
  field, Lewin's 44
  Kleinian 44
  leadership 7, 8
    see also under ACL
  organisation 1
  relevance to practice back at work 21
  sessions 6, 93
Therapeutic community 1, 2, 4, 64, 65, 66, 70

Therapy   66, 67, 69
  behaviour   110
Toleration of feelings   46
  anxiety   46, 47
Training-group
  Coverdale   19, 20, 24, 33, 108, 112
  prison officers   70-9
  trainers   70
  transfer of   88, 101, 126
Transaction   64, 131
Transferability, idea of   65, 68
Trust   79
Truth about   105, 108
  relative to method   108
'Truth, scientific'   133

Unconscious
  images   45
  processes   58
Unexpressed, or hidden, material   86, 120-1

Understanding, or grasp of
  what happens   104-8, 112
  and insight, strong sense   107, 108
    weak sense   107
Uniqueness of method   117, 125
  of pattern in method   125
Unstructured group   2, 3
  see also Group

Value system
  changes in   67
  experimental   66, 67
  management   67
  permissive   66, 67
  protestant   66

W-activity   45-6, 47-8, 52, 53, 63, 134
'What has to be done'   29
WOT (Way of talking)   107-11, 113, 129